A
CONFESSION

A CONFESSION

Leo Tolstoy

Translated by
Aylmer Maude

DOVER PUBLICATIONS, INC.
Mineola, New York

Bibliographical Note

This Dover edition, first published in 2005, is an unabridged republication of *A Confession* from *A Confession and What I Believe,* originally published by Oxford University Press, London, 1921. *A Confession* was first circulated in Russia in 1882. A new introductory Note has been specially prepared for the present edition.

Library of Congress Cataloging-in-Publication Data

Tolstoy, Leo, graf, 1828–1910.
   [Ispoved'. English]
   A confession / Leo Tolstoy ; translated by Aylmer Maude.
     p. cm.
   Originally published: with What I believe. London : Oxford University Press, 1921.
   ISBN-13: 978-0-486-43851-1 (pbk.)
   ISBN-10: 0-486-43851-1 (pbk.)
     1. Christianity—Miscellanea. 2. Christian life. 3. Faith. 4. Tolstoy, Leo, graf, 1828–1910—Religion. I. Title.

BR124.T6513 2005
230—dc22

          2004056218

Manufactured in the United States by LSC Communications
43851110   2018
www.doverpublications.com

NOTE

"My question—that which at the age of fifty brought me to the verge of suicide—was the simplest of questions, lying in the soul of every man from the foolish child to the wisest elder: it was a question without answering which one cannot live, as I had found by experience. It was: "What will come of what I am doing today or shall do tomorrow?— What will come of my whole life?"
—Leo Tolstoy, *A Confession*

Born into a life of wealth and privilege in early nineteenth-century Russia, Leo Tolstoy (1828–1910) achieved worldly fame as the author of *Anna Karenina, War and Peace,* and other magnificent works of fiction. Despite his success as a writer, however, he suffered a profoundly depressive midlife crisis that brought him to the brink of suicide. Part of his depression seems to have originated in the carousing and excesses of his younger days. He was a heavy gambler, womanizer, liar, and thief. He was also a soldier, who fought in the Crimean War. These experiences are recalled in *A Confession:*

> I cannot think of those years without horror, loathing, and heartache. I killed men in war, and challenged men to duels in order to kill them; I lost at cards, consumed the labour of the peasants, sentenced them to punishments, lived loosely and deceived people. Lying, robbery, adultery of all kinds, drunkenness, violence, murder—there was no crime I did not commit, and for all that people praised my

conduct, and my contemporaries considered and consider me to be a comparatively moral man.

Perhaps even more central to Tolstoy's depression than his regret for the horrifying acts he committed in his younger days was the lack of meaning in his life. Although born into an Orthodox Christian family, he found the traditional trappings of organized religion unpalatable. He was repulsed by sacraments, church services, fasts, and the adoration of relics and icons. Moreover, radical ideas from the West had made inroads among Russian intellectuals, eroding support for established religion, and driving the development of an atheistic humanism. None of this satisfied him. In the depths of his depression, Tolstoy found that he could not live without a higher purpose. The thought of a godless universe, in which individual lives were meaningless, was insupportable. Without belief in God he could not live, yet he could not believe in God.

Searching for answers, Tolstoy read widely, from the classical philosophy of the Greeks to the works of Kant and Schopenhauer. The latter two philosophers demonstrated (at least to Tolstoy's satisfaction) that the existence of God could not be proved by reason. After much study and soul-searching, Tolstoy concluded that rational knowledge does not give the meaning of life. In the face of a purposeless existence, the only rational choice is suicide. Yet, he could not bring himself to take that way out. Instead, the anguished thinker began to consider the simple, unquestioning faith of the Russian peasant. Observing that faith gave a meaning to life for these vast multitudes, he eventually came to the belief that faith alone "stores the deepest human wisdom," and faith alone makes it possible to live. As he puts it in *A Confession:* "I returned to a belief in God, in moral perfection, and in a tradition transmitting the meaning of life."

Gradually, Tolstoy formulated his own version of Christian philosophy, one that adhered closely to Christ's central message of love and compassion for all, and nonresistance to aggression and evil. He also put great emphasis on fair treatment of the poor and working class. For his pains, Tolstoy was excommunicated by the Russian Orthodox Church in 1901. By this time, however, his religious writings had won him a reputation as a sage and moral leader, and people from all over the world flocked to his estate, Yasnaya Polyana, in the Tula region south of Moscow. In his final years, the author took his Christian beliefs to an extreme level, renouncing his estate and trying to live as a poor, wandering ascetic.

Tolstoy's spiritual teachings influenced the nonviolent philosophy of such leaders as Gandhi, the kibbutz movement in Palestine, anarchism, and other ideologies. The chief value of *A Confession*, however, lies in its honest, unsparing and inspirational story of one man's search for inner peace. First distributed in 1882, it is translated here by Aylmer Maude, a respected translator and intimate of Tolstoy. The book provides a deeply personal firsthand view of the great author's spiritual struggle, his missteps and misgivings, years of doubt and discouragement, and final attainment of religious certainty and deep faith, based on strict adherence to the teachings of Christ.

I

I WAS baptized and brought up in the Orthodox Christian faith. I was taught it in childhood and throughout my boyhood and youth. But when I left the second course of the university, at the age of eighteen, I no longer believed any of the things I had been taught.

Judging by certain memories, I never seriously believed, but had merely relied on what I was taught and on what was professed by the grown-up people around me; and that reliance was very unstable.

I remember that before I was eleven, a boy, Vladimir Milyutin (long since dead), a grammar school pupil, visited us one Sunday and announced as the latest novelty a discovery made at his school. This discovery was that there is no God, and that all we are taught about Him is a mere invention (this was in 1838). I remember how interested my elder brothers were in this news. They called me to their council, and we all, I remember, became very animated, and accepted the news as something very interesting and quite possible.

I remember also that when my elder brother, Dmitry, who was then at the university, suddenly, in the passionate way natural to him, devoted himself to religion and began to attend all the Church services, to fast and to lead a pure and moral life, we all—even our elders—unceasingly held him up to ridicule and called him, for some unknown reason, "Noah." I remember that Musin-Pushkin, the then curator of Kazan University, when inviting us to a dance at his house, ironically persuaded my brother (who was declining the invitation) by the argument that even David danced before the Ark. I sympathized with these jokes made by my elders, and drew from them the conclusion that though it is necessary to learn the catechism and go to church, one must not take such things too seriously. I remember also that I read Voltaire when I was very young, and that his raillery, far from shocking me, amused me very much.

My lapse from faith occurred as is usual among people on our level of education. In most cases, I think, it happens thus: a man lives like everybody else, on the basis of principles not merely having nothing in common with religious doctrine, but generally opposed to it; religious doctrine does not play a part in life, in intercourse with others it is never encountered, and in a man's own life he never has to reckon with it. Religious doctrine is professed far away from life and independently of it. If it is encountered, it is only as an external phenomenon disconnected from life.

By a man's life and conduct, then as now, it was and is quite impossible to judge whether he is a believer or not. If there be a difference between a man who publicly professes Orthodoxy and one who denies it, the difference is not in favour of the former. Then as now, the public profession and confession of Orthodoxy was chiefly met with among people who were dull and cruel, and who considered themselves very important. Ability, honesty, reliability, good-nature and moral conduct were often met with among unbelievers.

The schools teach the catechism and send the pupils to church; and Government officials must produce certificates of having received Communion. But a man of our circle, who has finished his education and is not in the Government service, may even now (and formerly it was still easier for him to do so) live for ten or twenty years without once remembering that he is living among Christians and is himself reckoned a member of the Orthodox Christian Church.

So that, now as formerly, religious doctrine, accepted on trust and supported by external pressure, thaws away gradually under the influence of knowledge and experience of life which conflict with it, and a man very often lives on, imagining that he still holds intact the religious doctrine imparted to him in childhood, whereas in fact not a trace of it remains.

S., a clever and truthful man, once told me the story of how he ceased to believe. When he was already twenty-six, he once, on a hunting expedition, at the place where they put up for the night, by habit retained from childhood, knelt down in the evening to pray. His elder brother, who was at the hunt with him, was lying on some hay and watching him. When S. had finished and was settling down for the night, his brother said to him: "So you still do that?"

They said nothing more to one another. But from that day S. ceased to say his prayers or go to church. And now he has not prayed, received Communion, or gone to church for thirty years. And this not because he knows his brother's convictions and has joined him in them, nor because he has decided anything in his own soul, but simply because the word spoken by his brother was like the push of a finger on a wall that was ready to fall by its own weight. The word only showed that where he thought there was faith, in reality there had long been an empty place, and that therefore the utterance of words and the making of signs of the cross and genuflections while praying were quite senseless actions. Becoming conscious of their senselessness, he could not continue them.

So it has been and is, I think, with the great majority of people. I am speaking of people of our educational level, who are sincere with themselves, and not of those who make the profession of faith a means of attaining worldly aims. (Such people are the most fundamental infidels, for if faith is for them a means of attaining any worldly aims, then certainly it is not faith.) These people of our education are so placed that the light of knowledge and life has caused an artificial erection to melt away, and they have either already noticed this and swept its place clear, or they have not yet noticed it.

The religious doctrine taught me from childhood disappeared in me as in others, but with this difference, that as from the age of fifteen I began to read philosophical works, my rejection of the doctrine became a conscious one at a very early age. From the time I was sixteen I ceased to say my prayers and ceased to go to church or to fast, of my own volition. I did not believe what had been taught me in childhood, but I believed in something. What it was I believed in I could not at all have said. I believed in a God, or rather I did not deny God; but I could not have said what sort of God. Neither did I deny Christ and his teaching, but what his teaching consisted in I again could not have said.

Looking back on that time, I now see clearly that my faith—my only real faith—that which, apart from my animal instincts, gave impulse to my life—was a belief in perfecting myself. But in what this perfecting consisted, and what its object was, I could not have said. I tried to perfect myself mentally—I studied everything I could, anything life threw in my way; I tried to perfect my will, I drew up rules which I tried to follow; I perfected myself physically, cultivating my strength and agility by all sorts of exercises, and accustoming myself to endurance and patience by all kinds of privations. And all this I considered to be the pursuit of perfection. The beginning of it all was, of course, moral perfection; but that was soon replaced by perfection in general: by the desire to be better, not in my own eyes or those of God, but in the eyes of other people. And very soon this effort again changed into a desire to be stronger than others: to be more famous, more important and richer than others.

II

SOME day I will narrate the touching and instructive history of my life during those ten years of my youth. I think very many people have had the same experience. With all my soul I wished to be good; but I was young, passionate, and alone, completely alone when I sought goodness. Every time I tried to express my most sincere desire, which was to be morally good, I met with contempt and ridicule; but as soon as I yielded to low passions I was praised and encouraged.

Ambition, love of power, covetousness, lasciviousness, pride, anger and revenge—were all respected.

Yielding to those passions, I became like the grown-up folk, and I felt that they approved of me. The kind aunt with whom I lived, herself the purest of beings, always told me that there was nothing she so desired for me as that I should have relations with a married woman: '*Rien ne forme un jeune homme, comme une liaison avec une femme comme il faut.*'[1] Another happiness she desired for me was that I should become an aide-de-camp, and if possible aide-de-camp to the Emperor. But the greatest happiness of all would be that I should marry a very rich girl and so become possessed of as many serfs as possible.

I cannot think of those years without horror, loathing,

---

[1] Nothing so forms a young man, as an intimacy with a woman of good breeding.

and heartache. I killed men in war, and challenged men to duels in order to kill them; I lost at cards, consumed the labour of the peasants, sentenced them to punishments, lived loosely and deceived people. Lying, robbery, adultery of all kinds, drunkenness, violence, murder—there was no crime I did not commit, and for all that people praised my conduct, and my contemporaries considered and consider me to be a comparatively moral man.

So I lived for ten years.

During that time I began to write from vanity, covetousness, and pride. In my writings I did the same as in my life. To get fame and money, for the sake of which I wrote, it was necessary to hide the good and to display the evil. And I did so. How often in my writings I contrived to hide under the guise of indifference, or even of banter, those strivings of mine towards goodness, which gave meaning to my life! And I succeeded in this, and was praised.

At twenty-six years of age[2] I returned to Petersburg after the war, and met the writers. They received me as one of themselves and flattered me. And before I had time to look round I had adopted the views on life of the set of authors I had come among, and these views completely obliterated all my former strivings to improve. Those views furnished a theory which justified the dissoluteness of my life.

The view of life of these people, my comrades in authorship, consisted in this: that life in general goes on developing, and in this development we—men of thought—have the chief part; and among men of thought it is we—artists and poets—who have the greatest influence. Our vocation is to teach mankind. And lest the simple question should suggest itself: What do I know, and what can I teach? it was explained

---

[2] Tolstoy makes a slip here: he was twenty-seven.

in this theory that this need not be known, and that the artist and poet teach unconsciously. I was considered an admirable artist and poet, and therefore it was very natural for me to adopt this theory. I, artist and poet, wrote and taught, without myself knowing what. For this I was paid money; I had excellent food, lodging, women, and society; and I had fame, which showed that what I taught was very good.

This faith in the meaning of poetry and in the development of life was a religion, and I was one of its priests. To be its priest was very pleasant and profitable. And I lived a considerable time in this faith without doubting its validity. But in the second, and especially in the third year of this life, I began to doubt the infallibility of this religion and to examine it. My first cause of doubt was that I began to notice that the priests of this religion were not all in accord among themselves. Some said: We are the best and most useful teachers; we teach what is needed, but the others teach wrongly. Others said: No! we are the real teachers, and you teach wrongly. And they disputed, quarrelled, abused, cheated, and tricked one another. There were also many among us who did not care who was right and who was wrong, but were simply bent on attaining their covetous aims by means of this activity of ours. All this obliged me to doubt the validity of our creed.

Moreover, having begun to doubt the truth of the authors' creed itself, I also began to observe its priests more attentively, and I became convinced that almost all the priests of that religion, the writers, were immoral, and for the most part men of bad, worthless character, much inferior to those whom I had met in my former dissipated and military life; but they were self-confident and self-satisfied as only those can be who are quite holy or who do not know what holiness is. These people revolted me, I became revolting to myself, and I realized that that faith was a fraud.

But strange to say, though I understood this fraud and renounced it, yet I did not renounce the rank these people gave me: the rank of artist, poet, and teacher. I naïvely imagined that I was a poet and artist and could teach everybody without myself knowing what I was teaching, and I acted accordingly.

From my intimacy with these men I acquired a new vice: abnormally developed pride, and an insane assurance that it was my vocation to teach men, without knowing what.

To remember that time, and my own state of mind and that of those men (though there are thousands like them today), is sad and terrible and ludicrous, and arouses exactly the feeling one experiences in a lunatic asylum.

We were all then convinced that it was necessary for us to speak, write, and print as quickly as possible and as much as possible, and that it was all wanted for the good of humanity. And thousands of us, contradicting and abusing one another, all printed and wrote—teaching others. And without remarking that we knew nothing, and that to the simplest of life's questions: What is good and what is evil? we did not know how to reply, we all not listening to one another, talked at the same time, sometimes backing and praising one another in order to be backed and praised in turn, sometimes getting angry with one another—just as in a lunatic asylum.

Thousands of workmen laboured to the extreme limit of their strength day and night, setting the type and printing millions of words which the post carried all over Russia, and we still went on teaching and could in no way find time to teach enough, and were always angry that sufficient attention was not paid us.

It was terribly strange, but is now quite comprehensible. Our real innermost concern was to get as much money and praise as possible. To gain that end we could do nothing except write books and papers. So we did that. But in order to do such useless work and to feel assured that we were very important people, we required a theory justifying our activity. And so among us this theory was devised: "All that exists is reasonable. All that exists develops. And it all develops by means of Culture. And Culture is measured by the circulation of books and newspapers. And we are paid money and are respected because we write books and newspapers, and therefore we are the most useful and the best of men." This theory would have been all very well if we had been unanimous, but as every thought expressed by one of us was always met by a diametrically opposite thought expressed by another, we ought to have been driven to reflection. But we ignored this; people paid us money, and those on our side praised us; so each of us considered himself justified.

It is now clear to me that this was just as in a lunatic asylum; but then I only dimly suspected this, and like all lunatics, simply called all men lunatics except myself.

III

So I lived abandoning myself to this insanity for another six years, till my marriage. During that time I went abroad. Life in Europe and my acquaintance with leading and learned Europeans[1] confirmed me yet more in the faith in which I believed, of striving after perfection, for I found the same faith among them. That faith took with me the common form it assumes with the majority of educated people of our day. It was expressed by the word

---

[1] Russians generally make a distinction between Europeans and Russians.

"progress." It then appeared to me that this word meant
something. I did not as yet understand that, being tormented (like every live man) by the question how it is best
for me to live, in my answer, "Live in conformity with
progress," I was replying as a man in a boat would do if
when carried along by wind and waves he replied to what
for him was the chief and only question. "whither to
steer," by saying, "We are being carried somewhere."

I did not then notice this. Only occasionally—not by reason but by instinct—I revolted against this superstition, so
common in our day, by which people hide from themselves
their lack of understanding of life. . . . So, for instance, during my stay in Paris, the sight of an execution revealed to me
the instability of my superstitious belief in progress. When I
saw the head part from the body, and how they thumped
separately into the box, I understood, not with my mind but
with my whole being, that no theory of the reasonableness
of our present progress could justify this deed; and that
though everybody from the creation of the world, on whatever theory, had held it to be necessary, I knew it to be
unnecessary and bad; and therefore the arbiter of what is
good and evil is not what people say and do, nor is it
progress, but it is my heart and I. Another instance of a realization that the superstitious belief in progress is insufficient
as a guide to life, was my brother's death. Wise, good, serious, he fell ill while still a young man, suffered for more than
a year, and died painfully, not understanding why he had
lived, and still less why he had to die. No theories could give
me, or him, any reply to these questions during his slow and
painful dying. But these were only rare instances of doubt,
and I actually continued to live professing a faith only in
progress. "All evolves and I evolve with it: and why it is that
I evolve with all things will be known some day." So I ought
to have formulated my faith at that time.

On returning from abroad I settled in the country, and chanced to occupy myself with peasant schools. This work was particularly to my taste, because in it I had not to face the falsity which had become obvious to me and stared me in the face when I tried to teach people by literary means. Here, also, I acted in the name of Progress, but I already regarded Progress itself critically. I said to myself: "In some of its developments Progress has proceeded wrongly; and with primitive peasant children one must deal in a spirit of perfect freedom, letting them choose what path of progress they please." In reality I was ever revolving round one and the same insoluble problem, which was: How to teach without knowing what to teach. In the higher spheres of literary activity I had realized that one could not teach without knowing what; for I saw that people all taught differently, and by quarrelling among themselves only succeeded in hiding their ignorance from one another. But here, with peasant children, I thought to evade this difficulty by letting them learn what they liked. It amuses me now, when I remember how I shuffled in trying to satisfy my desire to teach, while in the depth of my soul I knew very well that I could not teach anything needful for I did not know what was needful. After spending a year at school work, I went abroad a second time, to discover how to teach others while myself knowing nothing.

And it seemed to me that I had learnt this abroad, and in the year of the peasants' emancipation (1861) I returned to Russia armed with all this wisdom; and having become an Arbiter,[2] I began to teach, both the uneducated peasants in schools and the educated classes through a maga-

---

[2] To keep peace between peasants and owners.

zine I published. Things appeared to be going well, but I felt I was not quite sound mentally, and that matters could not long continue in that way. And I should perhaps then have come to the state of despair I reached fifteen years later, had there not been one side of life still unexplored by me, which promised me happiness: that was marriage.

For a year I busied myself with arbitration work, the schools, and the magazine; and I became so worn out—as a result especially of my mental confusion—and so hard was my struggle as Arbiter, so obscure the results of my activity in the schools, so repulsive my shuffling in the magazine (which always amounted to one and the same thing: a desire to teach everybody, and to hide the fact that I did not know what to teach), that I fell ill, mentally rather than physically, threw up everything, and went away to the Bashkirs in the steppes, to breathe fresh air, drink kumys,[3] and live a merely animal life.

Returning from there I married. The new conditions of happy family life completely diverted me from all search for the general meaning of life. My whole life was centred at that time in my family, wife and children, and therefore in care to increase our means of livelihood. My striving after self-perfection, for which I had already substituted a striving for perfection in general, i.e. Progress, was now again replaced by the effort simply to secure the best possible conditions for myself and my family.

So another fifteen years passed.

In spite of the fact that I now regarded authorship as of no importance, I yet, during those fifteen years, continued to write. I had already tasted the temptation of authorship: the temptation of immense monetary rewards and applause

---

[3] A fermented drink prepared from mare's milk.

for my insignificant work; and I devoted myself to it as a means of improving my material position, and of stifling in my soul all questions as to the meaning of my own life, or of life in general.

I wrote, teaching what was for me the only truth, that one should live so as to have the best for oneself and one's family.

So I lived; but five years ago something very strange began to happen to me. At first I experienced moments of perplexity and arrest of life, and though I did not know what to do or how to live; and I felt lost and became dejected. But this passed, and I went on living as before. Then these moments of perplexity began to recur oftener and oftener, and always in the same form. They were always expressed by the questions: What's it for? What does it lead to?

At first it seemed to me that these were aimless and irrelevant questions. I thought that it was all well known, and that if I should ever wish to deal with the solution, it would not cost me much effort; just at present I had no time for it, but when I wanted to I should be able to find the answer. The questions, however, began to repeat themselves frequently, and more and more insistently to demand replies; and like drops of ink always falling on one place, they ran together into one black blot.

That occurred which happens to every one sickening with a mortal internal disease. At first trivial signs of indisposition appear, to which the sick man pays no attention; then these signs reappear more and more often and merge into one uninterrupted period of suffering. The suffering increases, and before the sick man can look round, what he took for a mere indisposition has already become more important to him than anything else in the world—it is death!

That was what happened to me. I understood that it was

no casual indisposition, but something very important, and that if these questions constantly repeated themselves, they would have to be answered. And I tried to answer them. The questions seemed such stupid, simple, childish questions; but as soon as I touched them and tried to solve them, I at once became convinced, (1) that they are not childish and stupid, but the most important and profound of life's questions; and (2) that, try as I would, I could not solve them. Before occupying myself with my Samara estate, the education of my son, or the writing of a book, I had to know *why* I was doing it. As long as I did not know why, I could do nothing, and could not live. Amid the thoughts of estate management which greatly occupied me at that time, the question would suddenly occur to me: "Well, you will have 6,000 *desyatinas*[4] of land in Samara Government and 300 horses, and what next?" . . . And I was quite disconcerted, and did not know what to think. Or when considering my plans for the education of my children, I would say to myself: "What for?" Or when considering how the peasants might become prosperous, I suddenly said to myself: "But what does it matter to me?" Or when thinking of the fame my works would bring me, I said to myself, "Very well; you will be more famous than Gogol or Pushkin or Shakespeare or Molière, or than all the writers in the world—and what of it?" And I could find no reply at all. The questions would not wait, they had to be answered at once, and if I did not answer them, it was impossible to live. But there was no answer.

I felt that what I had been standing on had collapsed, and that I had nothing left under my feet. What I had lived on no longer existed; and there was nothing left to live on.

---

[4] The *desyatina* is about 2¾ acres.

IV

MY life came to a standstill. I could breathe, eat, drink, and sleep, and I could not help doing these things; but there was no life, for there were no wishes the fulfilment of which I could consider reasonable. If I desired anything, I knew in advance that whether I satisfied my desire or not, nothing would come of it. Had a fairy come and offered to fulfil my desires I should not have known what to ask. If in moments of intoxication I felt something which, though not a wish, was a habit left by former wishes, in sober moments I knew this to be a delusion, and that there was really nothing to wish for. I could not even wish to know the truth, for I guessed of what it consisted. The truth was that life is meaningless. I had, as it were, lived, lived, and walked, walked, till I had come to a precipice and saw clearly that there was nothing ahead of me but destruction. It was impossible to stop, impossible to go back, and impossible to close my eyes or avoid seeing that there was nothing ahead but suffering and real death—complete annihilation.

It had come to this, that I, a healthy, fortunate man, felt I could no longer live: some irresistible power impelled me to rid myself one way or other of life. I cannot say I *wished* to kill myself. The power which drew me away from life was stronger, fuller, and more widespread than any mere wish. It was a force similar to the former striving to live, only in a contrary direction. All my strength drew me away from life. The thought of self-destruction now came to me as naturally as thoughts of how to improve my life had come formerly. And it was seductive that I had to be wily with myself lest I should carry it out too hastily. I did not wish to hurry, only because I wanted to use all efforts to disentangle the matter. "If I cannot unravel matters, there will always be time." And it was then that I, a man favoured by fortune, hid a cord from myself, lest I should hang myself from the crosspiece of the partition in my room, where I undressed alone every evening; and I ceased to go out shooting with a gun, lest I should be tempted by so easy a way of ending my life. I did not myself know what I wanted: I feared life, desired to escape from it; yet still hoped something of it.

And all this befell me at a time when all around me I had what is considered complete good fortune. I was not yet fifty; I had a good wife who loved me and whom I loved, good children, and a large estate which without much effort on my part improved and increased. I was respected by my relations and acquaintances more than at any previous time. I was praised by others, and without much self-deception could consider that my name was famous. And far from being insane or mentally diseased, I enjoyed on the contrary a strength of mind and body such as I have seldom met with among men of my kind; physically, I could keep up with the peasants at mowing, and mentally I could work for eight and ten hours at a stretch without experiencing any ill results from such exertion. And in this situation I came to this—that I could not live, and, fearing death, had to employ cunning with myself to avoid taking my own life.

My mental condition presented itself to me in this way: my life is a stupid and spiteful joke some one has played on me. Though I did not acknowledge a "some one" who created me, yet such a presentation—that some one had played an evil and stupid joke on me by placing me in the world—was the form of expression that suggested itself most naturally to me.

Involuntarily it appeared to me that there, somewhere, was some one who amused himself by watching how I lived

for thirty or forty years: learning, developing, maturing in
body and mind, and how—having with matured mental
powers reached the summit of life from which it all lay
before me, I stood on that summit—like an arch-fool—seeing clearly that there is nothing in life, and that there has
been and will be nothing. And *he* was amused. . . .

But whether that "some one" laughing at me existed or
not, I was none the better off. I could give no reasonable
meaning to any single action, or to my whole life. I was
only surprised that I could have avoided understanding
this from the very beginning—it has been so long known to
all. Today or tomorrow sickness and death will come (they
had come already) to those I love or to me; nothing will
remain but stench and worms. Sooner or later my affairs,
whatever they may be, will be forgotten, and I shall not
exist. Then why go on making any effort? . . . How can man
fail to see this? And how go on living? That is what is sur-
prising! One can only live while one is intoxicated with life;
as soon as one is sober it is impossible not to see that it is
all a mere fraud and a stupid fraud! That is precisely what
it is: there is nothing either amusing or witty about it: it is
simply cruel and stupid.

There is an Eastern fable, told long ago, of a traveller
overtaken on a plain by an enraged beast. Escaping from
the beast he gets into a dry well, but sees at the bottom of
the well a dragon that has opened its jaws to swallow him.
And the unfortunate man, not daring to climb out lest he
should be destroyed by the enraged beast, and not daring
to leap to the bottom of the well lest he should be eaten by
the dragon, seizes a twig growing in a crack in the well and
clings to it. His hands are growing weaker, and he feels he
will soon have to resign himself to the destruction that
awaits him above or below; but still he clings on. Then he
sees that two mice, a black and a white one, go regularly

round and round the stem of the twig to which he is clinging, and gnaw at it. And soon the twig itself will snap and
he will fall into the dragon's jaws. The traveller sees this
and knows that he will inevitably perish; but while still
hanging he looks around, sees some drops of honey on the
leaves of the twig, reaches them with his tongue and licks
them. So I too clung to the twig of life, knowing that the
dragon of death was inevitably awaiting me, ready to tear
me to pieces; and I could not understand why I had fallen
into such torment. I tried to lick the honey which formerly
consoled me; but the honey no longer gave me pleasure,
and the white and black mice of day and night gnawed at
the branch by which I hung. I saw the dragon clearly, and
the honey no longer tasted sweet. I only saw the
unescapable dragon and the mice, and I could not tear my
gaze from them. And this is not a fable, but the real unan-
swerable truth intelligible to all.

The deception of the joys of life which formerly allayed
my terror of the dragon now no longer deceived me. No
matter how often I may be told, "You cannot understand
the meaning of life, so do not think about it, but live," I can
no longer do it: I have already done it too long. I cannot
now help seeing day and night going round and bringing
me to death. That is all I see, for that alone is true. All else
is false.

The two drops of honey which diverted my eyes from
the cruel truth longer than the rest: my love of family, and
of writing—art as I called it—were no longer sweet to me.

"Family" . . . said I to myself. But my family—wife and
children—are also human. They are placed just as I am:
they must either live in a lie or see the terrible truth. Why
should they live? Why should I love them, guard them,
bring them up, or watch them? That they may come to the
despair that I feel, or else be stupid? Loving them, I can-

not hide the truth from them: each step in knowledge leads them to the truth. And the truth is death.

"Art, poetry?" . . . Under the influence of success and the praise of men, I had long assured myself that this was a thing one could do though death was drawing near—death which destroys all things, including my work and its remembrance; but soon I saw that that too was a fraud. It was plain to me that art is an adornment of life, an allurement to life. But life had lost its attraction for me, so how could I attract others? As long as I was not living my own life, but was borne on the waves of some other life—as long as I believed that life had a meaning, though one I could not express—the reflection of life in poetry and art of all kinds afforded me pleasure: it was pleasant to look at life in the mirror of art. But when I began to seek the meaning of life, and felt the necessity of living my own life, that mirror became for me unnecessary, superfluous, ridiculous, or painful. I could no longer soothe myself with what I now saw in the mirror, namely, that my position was stupid and desperate. It was all very well to enjoy the sight when in the depth of my soul I believed that my life had a meaning. Then the play of lights—comic, tragic, touching, beautiful, and terrible—in life amused me. But when I knew life to be meaningless and terrible, the play in the mirror could no longer amuse me. No sweetness of honey could be sweet to me when I saw the dragon, and saw the mice gnawing away my support.

Nor was that all. Had I simply understood that life had no meaning I could have borne it quietly, knowing that that was my lot. But I could not satisfy myself with that. Had I been like a man living in a wood from which he knows there is no exit, I could have lived; but I was like one lost in a wood who, horrified at having lost his way, rushes about, wishing to find the road. He knows that each step he takes confuses him more and more; but still he cannot help rushing about.

It was indeed terrible. And to rid myself of the terror I wished to kill myself. I experienced terror at what awaited me—knew that that terror was even worse than the position I was in; but still I could not patiently await the end. However convincing the argument might be that, in any case, some vessel in my heart would give way, or something would burst and all would be over, I could not patiently await that end. The horror of darkness was too great, and I wished to free myself from it as quickly as possible by noose or bullet. That was the feeling which drew me most strongly towards suicide.

V

"BUT perhaps I have overlooked something, or misunderstood something?" said I to myself several times. "It cannot be that this condition of despair is natural to man!" And I sought for an explanation of these problems in all the branches of knowledge acquired by men. I sought painfully and long, not from idle curiosity or listlessly, but painfully and persistently day and night—sought as a perishing man seeks for safety—and I found nothing.

I sought in all the sciences, but, far from finding what I wanted, became convinced that all who like myself had sought in knowledge for the meaning of life had equally found nothing. And not only had found nothing, but had plainly acknowledged that the very thing which made me despair—namely the senselessness of life—is the one indubitable thing man can know.

I sought everywhere; and thanks to a life spent in learning, and thanks also to my relations with the scholarly

world, I had access to scientists and scholars in all
branches of knowledge, and they readily showed me all
their knowledge, not only in books, but also in conversation, so that I had at my disposal all that science has to say
on this question of life.

I was long unable to believe that it gives no other reply
to life's questions than that which it actually does give. It
long seemed to me, when I saw the important and serious
air with which science announces its conclusions, which
have nothing in common with the real questions of human
life, that there was something I had not understood. I long
was timid before science, and it seemed to me that the lack
of conformity between the answers and my questions arose
not by the fault of science, but from my ignorance, but the
matter was for me not a game or an amusement, but one
of life and death, and I was involuntarily brought to the
conviction that my questions were the only legitimate
ones, forming the basis of all knowledge, and that not I
with my questions was to blame, but science if it pretends
to reply to those questions.

My question—that which at the age of fifty brought me
to the verge of suicide—was the simplest of questions,
lying in the soul of every man from the foolish child to the
wisest elder: it was a question without answering which
one cannot live, as I had found by experience. It was:
"What will come of what I am doing today or shall do
tomorrow?—What will come of my whole life?"

Differently expressed, the question is: "Why should I
live, why wish for anything, or do anything?" It can also be
expressed thus: "Is there any meaning in my life that the
inevitable death awaiting me does not destroy?"

To this one question, variously expressed, I sought an
answer in science. And I found that in relation to that
question all human knowledge is divided as it were into

two opposite hemispheres, at the ends of which are two poles: the one a negative, and the other a positive; but that neither at the one nor the other pole is the answer to life's questions.

The one series of sciences seems not to recognize the question, but clearly and exactly replies to its own independent questions: that is the series of experimental sciences, and at the extreme end of it stands mathematics. The other series of sciences recognizes the question, but does not answer it; that is the series of abstract sciences, and at the extreme end of them stands metaphysics.

From early youth I had been interested in the abstract sciences, but later the mathematical and natural sciences attracted me, and until I put my question definitely to myself, until that question had itself grown up within me urgently demanding a decision, I contented myself with those counterfeit answers which science gives.

Now in the experimental sphere I said to myself: "Everything develops and differentiates itself, moving towards complexity and perfection, and there are laws directing this movement. You are a part of the whole. Having learnt as far as possible the whole, and having learnt the law of evolution, you will understand also your place in the whole, and will know yourself." Ashamed as I am to confess it, there was a time when I seemed satisfied with that. It was just the time when I was myself becoming more complex and was developing. My muscles were growing and strengthening, my memory was being enriched, my capacity to think and understand was increasing, I was growing and developing; and feeling this growth in myself it was natural for me to think that such was the universal law in which I should find the solution of the question of my life. But a time came when the growth within me ceased. I felt that I was not developing, but fading, my muscles were weakening, my teeth falling out, and I saw that the law not only did not explain anything to me, but that there never had been or could be such a law, and that I had taken for a law what I had found in myself at a certain period of my life. I regarded the definition of that law more strictly; and it became clear to me that there could be no law of endless development; it became clear that to say, "in infinite space and time everything develops, becomes more perfect and more complex, is differentiated," is to say nothing at all. Those are all words with no meaning, for in the infinite there is neither complex nor simple, no forward nor backward, or better or worse.

Above all, my personal question, "What am I with my desires?" remained quite unanswered. And I understood that those sciences are very interesting, very attractive, but that they are exact and clear in inverse proportion to their applicability to the question of life: the less their applicability to the question of life, the more exact and clear they are, while the more they try to reply to the question of life, the more obscure and unattractive they become. If one turns to the division of sciences which attempt to reply to the questions of life—to physiology, psychology, biology, sociology—one encounters an appalling poverty of thought, the greatest obscurity, a quite unjustifiable pretension to solve irrelevant questions, and a continual contradiction of each authority by others and even by himself. If one turns to the branches of science which are not concerned with the solution of the questions of life, but which reply to their own special scientific questions, one is enraptured by the power of man's mind, but one knows in advance that they give no reply to life's questions. Those sciences simply ignore life's questions. They say: "To the question of what you are and why you live we have no reply, and are not occupied therewith; but if you want to know the laws of light, of chemical combinations, the laws of development of organisms, if you want to know the laws of bodies and their form, and the relation of numbers and quantities, if you want to know the laws of your mind, to all that we have clear, exact, and unquestionable replies."

In general the relation of the experimental sciences to life's question may be expressed thus: Question: "Why do I live?" Answer: "In infinite space, in infinite time, infinitely small particles change their forms in infinite complexity, and when you have understood the laws of those mutations of form, you will understand why you live on the earth."

Then in the sphere of abstract science I said to myself: "All humanity lives and develops on the basis of spiritual principles and ideals, which guide it. Those ideals are expressed in religions, in sciences, in arts, in forms of government. Those ideals become more and more elevated, and humanity advances to its highest welfare. I am part of humanity, and therefore my vocation is to forward the recognition and the realization of the ideals of humanity." And at the time of my weak-mindedness I was satisfied with that; but as soon as the question of life presented itself clearly to me, those theories immediately crumbled away. Not to speak of the unscrupulous obscurity with which those sciences announce conclusions formed on the study of a small part of mankind, as general conclusions; not to speak of the mutual contradictions of different adherents of this view, as to what are the ideals of humanity; the strangeness, not to say stupidity, of the theory consists in the fact that in order to reply to the question facing each man: "What am I?" or "Why do I live?" or "What must I do?" one has first to decide the question: "What is the life of the whole?" (which is to him unknown and of which he is acquainted with one tiny part in one minute period of time). To understand what he is, man must first understand all this mysterious humanity, consisting of people such as himself, who do not understand one another.

I have to confess that there was a time when I believed this. It was the time when I had my own favourite ideals justifying my own caprices, and I was trying to devise a theory which would allow one to consider my caprices as the law of humanity. But as soon as the question of life arose in my soul in full clearness that reply at once flew to dust. And I understood that as in the experimental sciences there are real sciences, and semi-sciences which try to give answers to questions beyond their competence, so in this sphere there is a whole series of most diffused sciences which try to reply to irrelevant questions. Semi-sciences of that kind, the juridical and the social-historical, endeavour to solve the questions of a man's life by pretending to decide, each in its own way, the question of the life of all humanity.

But as in the sphere of man's experimental knowledge one who sincerely inquires how he is to live cannot be satisfied with the reply—"Study in endless space the mutations, infinite in time and in complexity, of innumerable atoms, and then you will understand your life"—so also a sincere man cannot be satisfied with the reply: "Study the whole life of humanity of which we cannot know either the beginning or the end, of which we do not even know a small part, and then you will understand your own life." And like the experimental semi-sciences, so these other semi-sciences are the more filled with obscurities, inexactitudes, stupidities, and contradictions the further they diverge from the real problems. The problem of experimental science is the sequence of cause and effect in material phenomena. It is only necessary for experimental science to introduce the question of a final cause, and it becomes nonsensical. The problem of abstract science is the recognition of the primordial essence of life. It is only necessary to introduce the investigation of consequential phenomena (such as social and historical phenomena) and it also becomes nonsensical.

Experimental science then only gives positive knowledge and displays the greatness of the human mind when it does not introduce into its investigations the question of an ultimate cause. And, on the contrary, abstract science is only then science and displays the greatness of the human mind when it puts quite aside questions relating to the consequential causes of phenomena and regards man solely in relation to an ultimate cause. Such in this realm of science, forming the pole of the sphere, is metaphysics or philosophy. That science states the question clearly: "What am I, and what is the universe? And why do I exist, and why does the universe exist?" And since it has existed it has always replied in the same way. Whether the philosopher calls the essence of life existing within me, and in all that exists, by the name of "idea," or "substance," or "spirit," or "will," he says one and the same thing: that this essence exists, and that I am of the same essence; but why it is he does not know, and does not say, if he is an exact thinker. I ask: "Why should this essence exist? What results from the fact that it is and will be?" . . . And philosophy not merely does not reply, but is itself only asking that question. And if it is real philosophy, all its labour lies merely in trying to put that question clearly. And if it keeps firmly to its task, it cannot reply to the question otherwise than thus: "What am I, and what is the universe?" "All and nothing"; and to the question "Why?" by "I do not know."

So that however I may turn these replies of philosophy, I can never obtain anything like an answer—and not because, as in the clear experimental sphere, the reply does not relate to my question, but because here, though all the mental work is directed just to my question, there is no answer, but instead of an answer one gets the same question, only in a complex form.

VI

I N my search for answers to life's questions I experienced just what is felt by a man lost in a forest.

He reaches a glade, climbs a tree, and clearly sees the limitless distance, but sees that his home is not and cannot be there; then he goes into the dark wood, and sees the darkness, but there also his home is not.

So I wandered in that wood of human knowledge, amid the gleams of mathematical and experimental science which showed me clear horizons but in a direction where there could be no home, and also amid the darkness of the abstract sciences where I was immersed in deeper gloom the further I went, and where I finally convinced myself that there was, and could be, no exit.

Yielding myself to the bright side of knowledge, I understood that I was only diverting my gaze from the question. However alluringly clear those horizons which opened out before me might be, however alluring it might be to immerse oneself in the limitless expanse of those sciences, I already understood that the clearer they were the less they met my need and the less they applied to my question.

"I know," said I to myself, "what science so persistently tries to discover, and along that road there is no reply to the question as to the meaning of my life." In the abstract sphere I understood that notwithstanding the fact, or just because of the fact, that the direct aim of science is to reply to my question, there is no reply but that which I have myself already given: "What is the meaning of my life?" "There is none." Or: "What will come of my life?" "Nothing." Or: "Why does everything exist that exists, and why do I exist?" "Because it exists."

Enquiring for one region of human knowledge, I received an innumerable quantity of exact replies concerning matters about which I had not asked: about the chemical constituents of the stars, about the movement of the sun towards the constellation Hercules, about the origin of species and of man, about the forms of infinitely minute imponderable particles of ether; but in this sphere of knowledge the only answer to my question, "What is the meaning of my life?" was: "You are what you call your 'life'; you are a transitory, casual cohesion of particles. The mutual interactions and changes of these particles produce in you what you call your 'life.' That cohesion will last some time; afterwards the interaction of these particles will cease and what you call life' will cease, and so will all your questions. You are an accidentally united little lump of something. That little lump ferments. The little lump calls that fermenting its 'life'. The lump will disintegrate, and there will be an end of the fermenting and of all the questions." So answers the clear side of science and cannot answer otherwise if it strictly follows its principles.

From such a reply one sees that the reply does not answer the question. I want to know the meaning of my life, but that it is a fragment of the infinite, far from giving it a meaning, destroys its every possible meaning. The obscure compromises which that side of experimental exact science makes with abstract science, when it says that the meaning of life consists in development and in cooperation with development, owing to their inexactness and obscurity cannot be considered as replies.

The other side of science—the abstract side—when it

holds strictly to its principles, replying directly to the question, always replies, and in all ages has replied, in one and the same way: "The world is something infinite and incomprehensible. Human life is an incomprehensible part of that incomprehensible 'all'." Again I exclude all those compromises between abstract and experimental sciences which supply the whole ballast of the semi-sciences called juridical, political, and historical. In those semi-sciences the conception of development and progress is again wrongly introduced, only with this difference, that there it was the development of everything, while here it is the development of the life of mankind. The error is there as before: development and progress in infinity can have no aim or direction, and, as far as my question is concerned, no answer is given.

In truly abstract science, namely in genuine philosophy—not in that which Schopenhauer calls "professorial philosophy," which serves only to classify all existing phenomena in new philosophic categories and to call them by new names—where the philosopher does not lose sight of the essential question, the reply is always one and the same—the reply given by Socrates, Schopenhauer, Solomon, and Buddha.

"We approach truth only inasmuch as we depart from life," said Socrates when preparing for death. "For what do we, who love truth, strive after in life? To free ourselves from the body, and from all the evil that is caused by the life of the body! If so, then how can we fail to be glad when death comes to us?

"The wise man seeks death all his life, and therefore death is not terrible to him."

And Schopenhauer says:

"Having recognized the inmost nature of the world as *will*, and all its phenomena—from the unconscious working of the obscure forces of Nature up to the completely conscious action of man—as only the objectivity of that will, we shall by no means evade the consequence, that with the voluntary renunciation and surrender of the will, all those phenomena are also abolished: that constant stream and effort without end and without rest at all the grades of objectivity, in which and through which the world consists; the mutifarious forms succeeding each other in gradation; together with the form will disappear all the manifestations of will; and finally also the universal forms of this manifestation, time and space, and its last fundamental form: subject and object, all are abolished. Where there is no *will* there is no presentation, and no world. Before us, certainly, nothingness alone remains. But what resists this transition to nothingness, our nature, is indeed only that same will to live (Wille zum Leben), which we ourselves are, as it is our world. That we abhor annihilation so greatly, or, what is the same thing, our desire to live, is simply another expression of the fact that we strenuously will life, and are nothing but this will, and know nothing besides it. Therefore that which remains after the entire abolition of will, for us who are so full of will, is certainly nothing; but conversely, to those in whom the will has turned and has renounced itself, this our world, which is so real, with all its suns and milky ways—is nothing."

"Vanity of vanities," says Solomon—"vanity of vanities—all is vanity. What profit hath a man of all his labour which he taketh under the sun? One generation passeth away, and another generation cometh: but the earth abideth for ever. . . . The thing that hath been, is that which shall be; and that which is done is that which shall be done: and there is no new thing under the sun. Is there anything whereof it may be said, See, this is new? it hath been already of old time, which was before us. There is no remembrance of former things; neither shall there be any remembrance of things that are to come with those that shall come after. I the Preacher was King over Israel in Jerusalem. And I gave my heart to seek and search out by wisdom concerning all that is done under heaven: this sore travail hath God given to the sons of man to be exercised therewith. I have seen all the works that are done under the sun; and behold, all is vanity and vexation of spirit. . . . I communed with my own heart, saying, Lo, I am come to great estate, and have gotten more wisdom than all they that have been before me over Jerusalem: yea, my heart hath great experience of wisdom and knowledge. And I gave my heart to know wisdom, and to know madness and folly: I perceived that this also is vexation of spirit. For in much wisdom is much grief: and he that increaseth knowledge increaseth sorrow.

"I said in my heart, Go to now, I will prove thee with mirth, therefore enjoy pleasure: and behold this also is vanity. I said of laughter, It is mad: and of mirth, What doeth it? I sought in my heart how to cheer my flesh with wine, and while my heart was guided by wisdom, to lay hold on folly, till I might see what it was good for the sons of men that they should do under heaven the number of the days of their life. I made me great works; I builded me houses; I planted me vineyards; I made me gardens and orchards, and I planted trees in them of all kinds of fruits: I made me pools of water, to water therefrom the forest where trees were reared: I got me servants and maidens, and had servants born in my house; also I had great possessions of herds and flocks above all that were before me in Jerusalem: I gathered me also silver and gold and the peculiar treasure from kings and from the provinces: I got me men singers and women singers; and the delights of the sons of men, as musical instruments and that of all

sorts. So I was great, and increased more than all that were
before me in Jerusalem: also my wisdom remained with
me. And whatever mine eyes desired I kept not from
them. I withheld not my heart from any joy. . . . Then I
looked on all the works that my hands had wrought, and on
the labour that I had laboured to do: and, behold, all was
vanity and vexation of spirit, and there was no profit from
them under the sun. And I turned myself to behold wisdom, and madness, and folly. . . . But I perceived that one
even happeneth to them all. Then said I in my heart, As it
happeneth to the fool, so it happeneth even to me, and
why was I then more wise? Then I said in my heart, that
this also is vanity. For there is no remembrance of the wise
more than of the fool for ever; seeing that which now is in
the days to come shall all be forgotten. And how dieth the
wise man? as the fool. Therefore I hated life; because the
work that is wrought under the sun is grievous unto me: for
all is vanity and vexation of spirit. Yea, I hated all my labour
which I had taken under the sun: seeing that I must leave
it unto the man that shall be after me. . . . For what hath
man of all his labour, and of the vexation of his heart,
wherein he hath laboured under the sun? For all his days
are sorrows, and his travail grief; yea, even in the night his
heart taketh no rest. This is also vanity. Man is not blessed
with security that he should eat and drink and cheer his
soul from his own labour. . . . All things come alike to all:
there is one event to the righteous, and to the wicked; to
the good and to the evil; to the clean and to the unclean; to
him that sacrificeth, and to him that sacrificeth not; as is
the good, so is the sinner; and he that sweareth, as he that
feareth an oath. This is an evil in all that is done under the
sun, that there is one event unto all; yea, also the heart of
the sons of men is full of evil, and madness is in their heart
while they live, and after that they go to the dead. For him

that is among the living there is hope: for a living dog is better than a dead lion. For the living know that they shall die: but the dead know not any thing, neither have they any more a reward; for the memory of them is forgotten. Also their love, and their hatred, and their envy, is now perished; neither have they any more a portion for ever in any thing that is done under the sun."

So said Solomon, or whoever wrote those words.[1]

And this is what the Indian wisdom tells:

Sakya Muni, a young, happy prince, from whom the existence of sickness, old age, and death had been hidden, went out to drive and saw a terrible old man, toothless and slobbering. The prince, from whom till then old age had been concealed, was amazed, and asked his driver what it was, and how that man had come to such a wretched and disgusting condition, and when he learnt that this was the common fate of all men, that the same thing inevitably awaited him, the young prince, he could not continue his drive, but gave orders to go home, that he might consider this fact. So he shut himself up alone and considered it. And he probably devised some consolation for himself, for he subsequently again went out to drive, feeling merry and happy. But this time he saw a sick man. He saw an emaciated, livid, trembling man with dim eyes. The prince, from whom sickness had been concealed, stopped and asked what this was. And when he learnt that this was sickness, to which all men are liable, and that he himself, the healthy and happy prince, might himself fall ill tomorrow, he again was in no mood to enjoy himself, but gave orders

---

[1] Tolstoy's version differs slightly in a few places from our own Authorized or Revised version. I have followed his text, for in a letter to Fet, quoted on p. 11, vol. ii, of my *Life of Tolstoy*, he says that "The Authorized English version [of Ecclesiastes] is bad."

to drive home, and again sought some solace, and probably found it, for he drove out a third time for pleasure. But this third time he saw another new sight: he saw men carrying something. "What is that?" "A dead man." "What does *dead* mean?" asked the prince. He was told that to become dead means to become like that man. The prince approached the corpse, uncovered it, and looked at it. "What will happen to him now?" asked the prince. He was told that the corpse would be buried in the ground. "Why?" "Because he will certainly not return to life, and will only produce a stench and worms." "And is that the fate of all men? Will the same thing happen to me? Will they bury me, and shall I cause a stench and be eaten by worms?" "Yes." "Home! I shall not drive out for pleasure, and never will so drive out again!"

And Sakya Muni could find no consolation in life, and decided that life is the greatest of evils; and he devoted all the strength of his soul to free himself from it, and to free others; and to do this so that even after death, life shall not be renewed any more, but be completely destroyed at its very roots. So speaks all the wisdom of India.

These, then, are the direct replies that human wisdom gives, when it replies to life's question.

"The life of the body is an evil and a lie. Therefore the destruction of the life of the body is a blessing, and we should desire it," says Socrates.

"Life is that which should not be—an evil; and the passage into Nothingness is the only good in life," says Schopenhauer.

"All that is in the world—folly and wisdom and riches and poverty and mirth and grief—is vanity and emptiness. Man dies and nothing is left of him. And that is stupid," says Solomon.

"To live in the consciousness of the inevitability of suffering, of becoming enfeebled, of old age and of death, is impossible—we must free ourselves from life, from all possible life," says Buddha.

And what these strong minds said has been said and thought and felt by millions upon millions of people like them. And I have thought it and felt it.

So my wandering among the sciences, far from freeing me from my despair, only strengthened it. One kind of knowledge did not reply to life's question, the other kind replied directly confirming my despair, indicating not that the result at which I had arrived was the fruit of error or of a diseased state of my mind, but on the contrary, that I had thought correctly, and that my thoughts coincided with the conclusions of the most powerful of human minds.

It is no good deceiving oneself. It is all—vanity! Happy is he who has not been born: death is better than life, and one must free oneself from life.

VII

NOT finding an explanation in science, I began to seek for it in life, hoping to find it among the people around me. And I began to observe how the people around me—people like myself—lived, and what their attitude was to this question, which had brought me to despair.

And this is what I found among people who were in the same position as myself in regard to education and manner of life.

I found that for people of my circle there were four ways out of the terrible position in which we are all placed.

The first was that of ignorance. It consists in not knowing, not understanding, that life is an evil and an absurdity. People of this sort—chiefly women, or very young or very dull people—have not yet understood that question of life which presented itself to Schopenhauer, Solomon, and Buddha. They see neither the dragon that awaits them nor the mice gnawing the shrub by which they are hanging, and they lick the drops of honey. But they lick those drops of honey only for a while: something will turn their attention to the dragon and the mice, and there will be an end to their licking. From them I had nothing to learn—one cannot cease to know what one does know.

The second way out is epicureanism. It consists, while knowing the hopelessness of life, in making use meanwhile of the advantages one has, disregarding the dragon and the mice, and licking the honey in the best way, especially if there is much of it within reach. Solomon expresses this way out thus: "Then I commended mirth, because a man hath no better thing under the sun, than to eat, and to drink, and to be merry: and that this should accompany him in his labour the days of his life, which God giveth him under the sun.

"Therefore eat thy bread with joy and drink thy wine with a merry heart. . . . Live joyfully with the wife whom thou lovest all the days of the life of thy vanity . . . for this is thy portion in life and in thy labours which thou takest under the sun. . . . Whatsoever thy hand findeth to do, do it with thy might, for there is no work, nor device, nor knowledge, nor wisdom, in the grave, whither thou goest."

That is the way in which the majority of people of our circle make life possible for themselves. Their circumstances furnish them with more of welfare than of hardship, and their moral dullness makes it possible for them to forget that the advantage of their position is accidental, and that not everyone can have a thousand wives and palaces like Solomon, that for everyone who has a thousand wives there are a thousand without a wife, and that for each palace there are a thousand people who have to build it in the sweat of their brows; and that the accident that has today made me a Solomon may tomorrow make me a Solomon's slave. The dullness of these people's imagination enables them to forget the things that gave Buddha no peace—the inevitability of sickness, old age, and death, which today or tomorrow will destroy all these pleasures.

So think and feel the majority of people of our day and our manner of life. The fact that some of these people declare the dullness of their thoughts and imaginations to be a philosophy, which they call Positive, does not remove them, in my opinion, from the ranks of those who, to avoid seeing the question, lick the honey. I could not imitate these people; not having their dullness of imagination I could not artificially produce it in myself. I could not tear my eyes from the mice and the dragon, as no vital man can after he has once seen them.

The third escape is that of strength and energy. It consists, when one has understood that life is an evil and an absurdity, in destroying life. A few exceptionally strong and consistent people act so. Having understood the stupidity of the joke that has been played on them, and having understood that it is better to be dead than to be alive, and that it is best of all not to exist, they act accordingly and promptly end this stupid joke, since there are means: a rope round one's neck, water, a knife to stick into one's heart, or the trains on the railways; and the number of those of our circle who act in this way becomes greater and greater, and for the most part they act so at the best time of their life, when the strength of their mind is in full bloom, and few habits degrading man's mind have as yet been acquired.

I saw that this was the worthiest way of escape, and I wished to adopt it.

The fourth way out is that of weakness. It consists in seeing the truth of the situation, and yet clinging to life, knowing in advance that nothing can come of it. People of this
kind know that death is better than life, but, not having the
strength to act rationally—to end the deception quickly
and kill themselves—they seem to wait for something. This
is the escape of weakness, for if I know what is best, and it
is within my power, why not yield to what is best? . . . I found
myself in that category.

So people of my class evade the terrible contradiction in
four ways. Strain my attention as I would, I saw no way
except those four. One way was not to understand that life
is senseless, vanity, and an evil, and that it is better not to
live. I could not help knowing this, and when I once knew
it, could not shut my eyes to it. The second way was to use
life such as it is without thinking of the future. And I could
not do that. I, like Sakya Muni, could not ride out hunting
when I knew that old age, suffering, and death exist. My
imagination was too vivid. Nor could I rejoice in the
momentary accidents that for an instant threw pleasure to
my lot. The third way was, having understood that life is
evil and stupid, to end it by killing oneself. I understood
that, but somehow still did not kill myself. The fourth way
was to live like Solomon and Schopenhauer—knowing that
life is a stupid joke played upon us, and still to go on living,
washing oneself, dressing, dining, talking, and even writing
books. This was to me repulsive and tormenting, but I
remained in that position.

I see now that if I did not kill myself, it was due to some
dim consciousness of the invalidity of my thoughts.
However convincing and indubitable appeared to me the
sequence of my thoughts and of those of the wise, that
have brought us to the admission of the senselessness of

life, there remained in me a vague doubt of the justice of my conclusion.

It was like this: I, my reason, have acknowledged that life is senseless. If there is nothing higher than reason (and there is not: nothing can prove that there is), then reason is the creator of life for me. If reason did not exist, there would be for me no life. How can reason deny life, when it is the creator of life? Or to put it the other way: were there no life, my reason would not exist; therefore reason is life's son. Life is all. Reason is its fruit, yet reason rejects life itself! I felt that there was something wrong here.

Life is a senseless evil, that is certain, said I to myself. Yet I have lived and am still living, and all mankind lived and lives. How is that? Why does it live, when it is possible not to live? Is it that only I and Schopenhauer are wise enough to understand the senselessness and evil of life?

The reasoning showing the vanity of life is not so difficult, and has long been familiar to the very simplest folk; yet they have lived and still live. How is it they all live and never think of doubting the reasonableness of life?

My knowledge, confirmed by the wisdom of the sages, has shown me that everything on earth—organic and inorganic—is all most cleverly arranged—only my own position is stupid. And those fools—the enormous masses of people—know nothing about how everything organic and inorganic in the world is arranged; but they live, and it seems to them that their life is very wisely arranged! . . .

And it struck me: "But what if there is something I do not yet know? Ignorance behaves just in that way. Ignorance always says just what I am saying. When it does not know something, it says that what it does not know is stupid. Indeed, it appears that there is a whole humanity that lived and lives as if it understood the meaning of its life, for without understanding it it could not live; but I say that all this life is senseless and that I cannot live.

"Nothing prevents our denying life by suicide. Well then, kill yourself, and you won't discuss. If life displeases you, kill yourself! You live, and cannot understand the meaning of life—then finish it; and do not fool about in life, saying and writing that you do not understand it. You have come into good company, where people are contented and know what they are doing; if you find it dull and repulsive—go away!"

Indeed, what are we who are convinced of the necessity of suicide, yet do not decide to commit it, but the weakest, most inconsistent, and to put it plainly, the stupidest of men, fussing about with our own stupidity as a fool fusses about with a painted hussy? For our wisdom, however indubitable it may be, has not given us the knowledge of the meaning of our life. But all mankind, who sustain life—millions of them—do not doubt the meaning of life.

Indeed, from the most distant times of which I know anything, when life began, people have lived, knowing the argument about the vanity of life, which has shown me its senselessness, and yet they lived attributing some meaning to it.

From the time when any life began among men they had that meaning of life, and they led that life, which has descended to me. All that is in me and around me, all, corporeal and incorporeal, is the fruit of their knowledge of life. Those very instruments of thought with which I consider this life and condemn it were all devised not by me but by them. I myself was born, taught, and brought up thanks to them. They dug out the iron, taught us to cut down the forests, tamed the cows and horses, taught us to sow corn and to live together, organized our life, and taught me to think and speak. And I, their product, fed, supplied with drink, taught by them, thinking with their thoughts and words, have argued that they are an absurdity! "There is something wrong," said I to myself. "I have blundered somewhere." But where the mistake was, it was a long time before I could find out.

VIII

ALL these doubts, which I am now able to express more or less systematically, I could not then have expressed. I then only felt that however logically inevitable were my conclusions concerning the vanity of life, confirmed as they were by the greatest thinkers, there was something not right about them. Whether it was in the reasoning itself or in the statement of the question I did not know—I only felt that the conclusion was rationally convincing, but that that was insufficient. All these conclusions could not so convince me as to make me do what followed from my reasoning, that is to say, kill myself. And I should have told an untruth had I, without killing myself, said that reason had brought me to the point I had reached. Reason worked, but something else was also working which I can only call a consciousness of life. A force was working which compelled me to turn my attention to this and not to that; and it was this force which extricated me from my desperate situation and turned my mind in quite another direction. This force compelled me to turn my attention to the fact that I and a few hundred similar people are not the whole of mankind, and that I did not yet know the life of mankind.

Looking at the narrow circle of my equals, I saw only people who had not understood the question, or who had understood it and drowned it in life's intoxication, or had understood it and ended their lives, or had understood it and yet, from weakness, were living out their desperate life. And I saw no others. It seemed to me that that narrow circle of rich, learned, and leisured people to which I belonged formed the whole of humanity, and that those milliards of others who have lived and are living were cattle of some sort—not real people.

Strange, incredibly incomprehensible as it now seems to me, that I could, while reasoning about life, overlook the whole life of mankind that surrounded me on all sides; that I could to such a degree blunder so absurdly as to think that my life, and Solomon's and Schopenhauer's, is the real, normal life, and that the life of the milliards is a circumstance undeserving of attention—strange as this now is to me, I see that so it was. In the delusion of my pride of intellect, it seemed to me so indubitable that I and Solomon and Schopenhauer had stated the question so truly and exactly that nothing else was possible—so indubitable did it seem that all those milliards consisted of men who had not yet arrived at an apprehension of all the profundity of the question—that I sought for the meaning of my life without it once occurring to me to ask: "But what meaning is, and has been given to their lives by all the milliards of common folk who live and have lived in the world?"

I long lived in this state of lunacy, which, in fact if not in words, is particularly characteristic of us very liberal and learned people. But thanks either to the strange physical affection I have for the real labouring people, which compelled me to understand them and to see that they are not so stupid as we suppose, or thanks to the sincerity of my conviction that I could know nothing beyond the fact that the best I could do was to hang myself, at any rate I instinctively felt that if I wished to live and understand the meaning of life, I must seek this meaning not among those who have lost it and wish to kill themselves, but among those milliards of the past and the present who make life and who support the burden of their own lives and of ours also. And I considered the enormous masses of those simple, unlearned, and poor people who have lived and are living, and I saw something quite different. I saw that, with rare exceptions, all those milliards who have lived and are living do not fit into my divisions, and that I could not class them as not understanding the question, for they themselves state it, and reply to it with extraordinary clearness. Nor could I consider them epicureans, for their life consists more of privations and sufferings than of enjoyments. Still less could I consider them as irrationally dragging on a meaningless existence, for every act of their life as well as death itself is explained by them. To kill themselves they consider the greatest evil. It appeared that all mankind had a knowledge, unacknowledged and despised by me, of the meaning of life. It appeared that reasonable knowledge does not give the meaning of life, that it excludes life: while the meaning attributed to life by milliards of people, by all humanity, rests on some despised pseudo-knowledge.

Rational knowledge, presented by the learned and wise, denies the meaning of life, but the enormous masses of men, the whole of mankind, receive that meaning in irrational knowledge. And that irrational knowledge is faith, that very thing which I could not but reject. It is God, One in Three; the creation in six days; the devils and angels, and all the rest that I cannot accept as long as I retain my reason.

My position was terrible. I knew I could find nothing along the path of reasonable knowledge, except a denial of life; and there—in faith—was nothing but a denial of reason, which was yet more impossible for me than a denial of life. From rational knowledge it appeared that life is an evil, and people know this—it depends on them not to live; yet they lived and still live, and I myself live, though I have long known that life is senseless and an evil. By faith it appears that in order to understand the meaning of life I must repudiate my reason, the very thing for which alone a meaning is required.

IX

A CONTRADICTION arose from which there were two exits. Either that which I called reason was not so rational as I supposed, or that which seemed to me irrational was not so irrational as I supposed. And I began to verify the line of argument of my rational knowledge.

Verifying the line of argument of rational knowledge, I found it quite correct. The conclusion that life is nothing was inevitable; but I noticed a mistake. The mistake lay in this, that my reasoning was not in accord with the question I had put. The question was: "Why should I live, that is to say, what real, permanent result will come out of my illusory transitory life—what meaning has my finite existence in this infinite world?" And to reply to that question I had studied life.

The solution of all the possible questions of life could evidently not satisfy me, for my question, simple as it at first appeared, included a demand for an explanation of the finite in terms of the infinite, and vice versa.

I asked: "What is the meaning of my life, beyond time, cause, and space?" And I replied to the question: "What is the meaning of my life within time, cause, and space?" It resulted that, after long efforts of thought, I replied: "None."

In my reasonings I constantly compared (nor could I do otherwise) the finite with the finite, and the infinite with the infinite; but for that reason I reached the inevitable result: force is force, matter is matter, will is will, the infinite is the infinite, nothing is nothing—and that was all that could result.

It was something like what happens in mathematics, when, thinking to solve an equation, we find we are working on an identity. The line of reasoning is correct, but results in the answer that a equals a, or x equals x, or o equals o. The same thing happened with my reasoning in relation to the question of the meaning of my life. The replies given by all science to that question only result in—identity.

And really, strictly scientific knowledge—that knowledge which begins, as Descartes's did, with complete doubt about everything—rejects all knowledge admitted on faith, and builds everything afresh on the laws of reason and experience, and cannot give any other reply to the question of life than that which I obtained: an indefinite reply. Only at first had it seemed to me that knowledge had given a positive reply—the reply of Schopenhauer: that life has no meaning and is an evil. But on examining the matter I understood that the reply is not positive, it was only my feeling that so expressed it. Strictly expressed, as it is by the Brahmins and by Solomon and Schopenhauer, the reply is merely indefinite, or an identity: o equals o, life is nothing. So that philosophic knowledge denies nothing, but only replies that the question cannot be solved by it—that for it the solution remains indefinite.

Having understood this, I understood that it was not possible to seek in rational knowledge for a reply to my question, and that the reply given by rational knowledge is a mere indication that a reply can only be obtained by a different statement of the question, and only when the relation of the finite to the infinite is included in the question. And I understood that, however irrational and distorted might be the replies given by faith, they have this advantage, that they introduce into every answer a relation between the finite and the infinite, without which there can be no solution.

In whatever way I stated the question, that relation appeared in the answer. How am I to live?—According to the law of God. What real result will come of my life?—Eternal torment or eternal bliss. What meaning has life, that death does not destroy?—Union with the eternal God: heaven.

So that besides rational knowledge, which had seemed to me the only knowledge, I was inevitably brought to acknowledge that all live humanity has another irrational knowledge—faith which makes it possible to live. Faith still remained to me as irrational as it was before, but I could not but admit that it alone gives mankind a reply to the questions of life; and that consequently it makes life possible. Reasonable knowledge had brought me to acknowledge that life is senseless—my life had come to a halt and I wished to destroy myself. Looking around on the whole of mankind I saw that people live and declare that they know the meaning of life. I looked at myself, I had lived as long as I knew a meaning of life. As to others so also to me faith had given a meaning to life and had made life possible.

Looking again at people of other lands, at my contemporaries and at their predecessors, I saw the same thing. Where there is life there, since man began, faith has made life possible for him, and the chief outline of that faith is everywhere and always identical.

Whatever the faith might be, and whatever answers it might give, and to whomsoever it gives them, every such answer gives to the finite existence of man an infinite meaning, a meaning not destroyed by sufferings, deprivations, or death. This means that only in faith can we find for life a meaning and a possibility. What, then, is this faith? And I understood that faith is not merely "the evidence of things not seen," etc., and is not a revelation (that defines only one of the indications of faith), is not the relation of man to God (one has first to define faith and then God, and not define faith through God); it is not only agreement with what has been told one (as faith is most usually supposed to be), but faith is a knowledge of the meaning of human life in consequence of which man does not destroy himself but lives. Faith is the strength of life. If a man lives he believes in something. If he did not believe that one must live for something, he would not live. If he does not see and recognize the illusory nature of the finite, he believes in the finite; if he understands the illusory nature of the finite, he must believe in the infinite. Without faith he cannot live.

And I recalled the whole course of my mental labour and was horrified. It was now clear to me that for man to be able to live he must either not see the infinite, or have such an explanation of the meaning of life as will connect the finite with the infinite. Such an explanation I had had; but as long as I believed in the finite I did not need the explanation, and I began to verify it by reason. And in the light of reason the whole of my former explanation flew to atoms. But a time came when I ceased to believe in the finite. And then I began to build up on rational foundations, out of what I knew, an explanation which would give a meaning to life; but nothing could I build. Together with the best human intellects I reached the result that o equals o, and was much astonished at that conclusion, though nothing else could have resulted.

What was I doing when I sought an answer in the experimental sciences? I wished to know why I live, and for this purpose studied all that is outside me. Evidently I might learn much, but nothing of what I needed.

What was I doing when I sought an answer in philosophical knowledge? I was studying the thoughts of those who had found themselves in the same position as I, lacking a reply to the question "Why do I live?" Evidently I could learn nothing but what I knew myself, namely that nothing can be known.

What am I?—A part of the infinite. In those few words lies the whole problem.

Is it possible that humanity has only put that question to itself since yesterday? And can no one before me have set himself that question—a question so simple, and one that springs to the tongue of every wise child?

Surely that question has been asked since man began; and naturally, for the solution of that question since man began, it has been equally insufficient to compare the finite with the finite and the infinite with the infinite, and since man began the relation of the finite to the infinite has been sought out and expressed.

All these conceptions in which the finite has been adjusted to the infinite, and a meaning found for life: the conception of God, of will, of goodness, we submit to logical examination. And all those conceptions fail to stand reason's criticism.

Were it not so terrible, it would be ludicrous, with what pride and self-satisfaction we, like children, pull the watch to pieces, take out the spring, make a toy of it, and are then surprised that the watch does not go.

A solution of the contradiction between the finite and the infinite, and such a reply to the question of life as will make it possible to live, is necessary and precious. And that is the only solution which we find everywhere, always, and among all peoples: a solution descending from times in which we lose sight of the life of man, a solution so difficult that we can compose nothing like it—and this solution we light-heartedly destroy in order again to set the same question, which is natural to every one and to which we have no answer.

The conception of an infinite God, the divinity of the soul, the connexion of human affairs with God, the unity and existence of the soul, man's conception of moral goodness and evil—are conceptions formulated in the hidden infinity of human thought, they are those conceptions without which neither life nor I should exist; yet rejecting all that labour of the whole of humanity, I wished to remake it afresh myself and in my own manner.

I did not then think like that, but the germs of these thoughts were already in me. I understood, in the first place, that my position with Schopenhauer and Solomon, notwithstanding our wisdom, was stupid: we see that life is an evil and yet continue to live. That is evidently stupid, for if life is senseless, and I am so fond of what is reasonable, it should be destroyed, and then there would be no one to challenge it. Secondly, I understood that all one's reasonings turned in a vicious circle, like a wheel out of gear with its pinion. However much and however well we may reason, we cannot obtain a reply to the question; but o will always equal o, and therefore our path is probably erroneous. Thirdly, I began to understand that in the replies given by faith is stored up the deepest human wisdom, and that I had no right to deny them on the ground of reason, and that those answers are the only ones which reply to life's question.

X

I UNDERSTOOD this, but it made matters no better for me. I was now ready to accept any faith, if only it did not demand of me a direct denial of reason—which would be a falsehood. And I studied Buddhism and Mohammedanism from books, and most of all I studied Christianity both from books and from the people around me.

Naturally I first of all turned to the Orthodox of my circle, to people who were learned: to Church theologians, monks, to theologians of the newest shade, and even to Evangelicals, who profess salvation by belief in the Redemption. And I seized on these believers and questioned them as to their beliefs and their understanding of the meaning of life.

But though I made all possible concessions, and avoided all disputes, I could not accept the faith of these people. I saw that what they gave out as their faith did not explain the meaning of life but obscured it, and that they themselves affirm their belief, not to answer that question of life which brought me to faith, but for some other aims alien to me.

I remember the painful feeling of fear of being thrown back into my former state of despair, after the hope I often experienced in my intercourse with these people.

The more fully they explained to me their doctrines, the more clearly did I perceive their error and realized that my hope of finding in their belief an explanation of the meaning of life was vain.

It was not that in their doctrines they mixed many unnecessary and unreasonable things with the Christian truths that had always been near to me: that was not what repelled me. I was repelled by the fact that these people's lives were like my own, with only this difference—that such a life did not correspond to the principles they expounded in their teachings. I clearly felt that they deceived themselves and that they, like myself, found no other meaning in life than to live while life lasts, taking all one's hands can seize. I saw this because if they had had a meaning which destroyed the fear of loss, suffering, and death, they would not have feared these things. But they, these believers of our circle, just like myself, living in sufficiency and superfluity, tried to increase or preserve them, feared privations, suffering, and death, and just like myself and all of us unbelievers, lived to satisfy their desires, and lived just as badly, if not worse, than the unbelievers.

No arguments could convince me of the truth of their faith. Only deeds which showed that they saw a meaning in life, which made what was so dreadful to me—poverty, sickness, and death—not dreadful to them, could convince me. And such deeds I did not see among the various believers in our circle. On the contrary, I saw such deeds done[1] by people of our circle who were the most unbelieving, but never by our so-called believers.

And I understood that the belief of these people was not the faith I sought, and that their faith is not a real faith but an epicurean consolation in life.

I understood that that faith may perhaps serve, if not for a consolation at least for some distraction for a repentant Solomon on his death-bed, but it cannot serve for the great majority of mankind, who are called on not to amuse themselves while consuming the labour of others, but to create life.

For all humanity to be able to live, and continue to live attributing a meaning to life, they, those milliards, must have a different, a real, knowledge of faith. Indeed, it was not the fact that we, with Solomon and Schopenhauer, did not kill ourselves that convinced me of the existence of

---

[1] This passage is noteworthy as being one of the few references made by Tolstoy at this period to the revolutionary or "Back-to-the-People" movement, in which many young men and women were risking and sacrificing home, property, and life itself, from motives which had much in common with his own perception that the upper layers of Society are parasitic, and prey on the vitals of the people who support them.

faith, but the fact that those milliards of people have lived and are living, and have borne Solomon and us on the current of their lives.

And I began to draw near to the believers among the poor, simple, unlettered folk: pilgrims, monks, sectarians, and peasants. The faith of these common people was the same Christian faith as was professed by the pseudo-believers of our circle. Among them, too, I found a great deal of superstition mixed with the Christian truths; but the difference was that the superstitions of the believers of our circle were quite unnecessary to them, and were not in conformity with their lives, being merely a kind of epicurean diversion; but the superstitions of the believers among the labouring masses conformed so with their lives that it was impossible to imagine them to oneself without those superstitions, which were a necessary condition of their life. The whole life of believers in our circle was a contradiction of their faith, but the whole life of the working-folk believers was a confirmation of the meaning of life which their faith gave them. And I began to look well into the life and faith of these people, and the more I considered it the more I became convinced that they have a real faith, which is a necessity to them and alone gives their life a meaning and makes it possible for them to live. In contrast with what I had seen in our circle—where life without faith is possible, and where hardly one in a thousand, acknowledges himself to be a believer—among them there is hardly one unbeliever in a thousand. In contrast with what I had seen in our circle, where the whole of life is passed in idleness, amusement, and dissatisfaction, I saw that the whole life of these people was passed in heavy labour, and that they were content with life. In contradistinction to the way in which people of our circle oppose fate and complain of it on account of deprivations and sufferings, these people accepted illness and sorrow without any perplexity or opposition, and with a quiet and firm conviction that all is good. In contradistinction to us, who the wiser we are the less we understand the meaning of life, and see some evil irony in the fact that we suffer and die, these folk live and suffer, and they approach death and suffering with tranquillity and in most cases gladly. In contrast to the fact that a tranquil death, a death without horror and despair, is a very rare exception in our circle, a troubled, rebellious, and unhappy death is the rarest exception among the people. And such people, lacking all that for us and for Solomon is the only good of life, and yet experiencing the greatest happiness, are a great multitude. I looked more widely around me. I considered the life of the enormous mass of the people in the past and the present. And of such people, understanding the meaning of life and able to live and to die, I saw not two or three, or tens, but hundreds, thousands, and millions. And they all—endlessly different in their manners, minds, education, and position, as they were—all alike, in complete contrast to my ignorance, knew the meaning of life and death, laboured quietly, endured deprivations and sufferings, and lived and died, seeing therein not vanity but good.

And I learnt to love these people. The more I came to know their life, the life of those who are living and of others who are dead, of whom I read and heard, the more I loved them and the easier it became for me to live. So I went on for about two years, and a change took place in me which had long been preparing, and the promise of which had always been in me. It came about that the life of our circle, the rich and learned, not merely became distasteful to me, but lost all meaning in my eyes. All our actions, discussions, science and art, presented itself to me in a new light. I understood that it is all merely self-indulgence, and that to find a meaning in it is impossible; while the life of the whole labouring people, the whole of mankind who produce life, appeared to me in its true significance. I understood that *that* is life itself, and that the meaning given to that life is true: and I accepted it.

XI

AND remembering how those very beliefs had repelled me and had seemed meaningless when professed by people whose lives conflicted with them, and how these same beliefs attracted me and seemed reasonable when I saw that people lived in accord with them, I understood why I had then rejected those beliefs and found them meaningless, yet now accepted them and found them full of meaning. I understood that I had erred, and why I erred. I had erred not so much because I thought incorrectly, as because I lived badly. I understood that it was not an error in my thought that had hid truth from me, as much as my life itself in the exceptional conditions of epicurean gratification of desires in which I passed it. I understood that my question as to what my life is, and the answer, an evil, was quite correct. The only mistake was that the answer referred only to my life; but I had referred it to life in general. I asked myself what my life is, and got the reply: An evil and an absurdity. And really my life—a life of indulgence of desires—was senseless and evil, and therefore the reply, "Life is evil and an absurdity," referred only to my life, but not to human life in general. I understood the truth, which I afterwards found in the Gospels, "that men loved darkness rather than the light, for their works were evil. For everyone that doeth ill hateth the light, and cometh not to the light, lest his works should be reproved."

I perceived that to understand the meaning of life it is necessary first that life should not be meaningless and evil, and then reason is needed to explain it. I understood why I had so long wandered round so evident a truth, and that if one is to think and speak of the life of mankind, one must think and speak of that life, and not of the life of some of life's parasites. That truth was always as true as that two and two are four, but I had not acknowledged it, because on admitting two and two to be four, I had also to admit that I was bad; and to feel myself to be good was for me more important and necessary than for two and two to be four. I came to love good people, hated myself, and confessed the truth. Now all became clear to me.

What if an executioner passing his whole life in torturing people and cutting off their heads—or a hopeless drunkard, or a madman settled for life in a dark room which he has fouled, and imagined that he would perish if he left—what if he asked himself: "What is life?" Evidently he could get no other reply to that question than that life is the greatest evil; and the madman's answer would be perfectly correct, but only as applied to himself. What if I am such a madman? What if all we rich and leisured people are such madmen? and I understood that we are really such madmen. I at any rate was certainly such.

And indeed a bird is so made that it must fly, collect food, and build a nest, and when I see that a bird does this, I have pleasure in its joy. A goat, a hare, and a wolf are so made that they must feed themselves, and must breed and feed their family, and when they do so, I feel firmly assured that they are happy and that their life is a reasonable one. Then what should a man do? He too should produce his living as the animals do, but with this difference, that he will perish if he does it alone; he must obtain it not for himself but for all. And when he does that, I have a firm assurance that he is happy and that his life is reasonable. But what had I done during the whole thirty years of my responsible life? Far from producing sustenance for all, I did not even produce it for myself. I lived as a parasite, and on asking myself, what is the use of my life? I got the reply: "No use." If the meaning of human life lies in supporting it, how could I—who for thirty years had been engaged not in supporting life but on destroying it in myself and in others—how could I obtain any other answer than that my life was senseless and an evil? . . . It was both senseless and evil.

The life of the world endures by some one's will—by the life of the whole world and by our lives some one fulfils his purpose. To hope to understand the meaning of that will one must first perform it by doing what is wanted of us. But if I will not do what is wanted of me, I shall never understand what is wanted of me, and still less what is wanted of us all and of the whole world.

If a naked, hungry beggar has been taken from the cross-roads, brought into a building belonging to a beautiful establishment, fed, supplied with drink, and obliged to move a handle up and down, evidently, before discussing why he was taken, why he should move the handle, and whether the whole establishment is reasonably arranged—the beggar should first of all move the handle. If he moves the handle, he will understand that it works a pump, that the pump draws water and that the water irrigates the garden beds; then he will be taken from the pumping station to another place where he will gather fruits and will enter into the joy of his master, and, passing from lower to higher work, will understand more and more of the arrangements of the establishment, and taking part in it will never think of asking why he is there, and will certainly not reproach the master.

So those who do his will, the simple, unlearned working folk, whom we regard as cattle, do not reproach the master; but we, the wise, eat the master's food but do not do what the master wishes, and instead of doing it sit in a circle and discuss: "Why should that handle be moved? Isn't it stupid!" So we have decided. We have decided that the master is stupid, or does not exist, and that we are wise, only we feel that we are quite useless and that we must somehow do away with ourselves.

XII

THE consciousness of the error in reasonable knowledge helped me to free myself from the temptation of idle ratiocination. The conviction that knowledge of truth can only be found by living led me to doubt the rightness of my life; but I was saved only by the fact that I was able to tear myself from my exclusiveness and to see the real life of the plain working people, and to understand that it alone is real life. I understood that if I wish to understand life and its meaning, I must not live the life of a parasite, but must live a real life, and—taking the meaning given to live by real humanity, and merging myself in that life—verify it.

During that time this is what happened to me. During that whole year, when I was asking myself almost every moment whether I should not end matters with a noose or a bullet—all that time, together with the course of thought and observation about which I have spoken, my heart was oppressed with a painful feeling, which I can only describe as a search for God.

I say that that search for God was not reasoning but a feeling, because that search proceeded not from the course of my thoughts—it was even directly contrary to them—but proceeded from the heart. It was a feeling of fear, orphanage, isolation in a strange land, and a hope of help from some one.

Though I was quite convinced of the impossibility of proving the existence of a Deity (Kant had shown, and I quite understood him, that it could not be proved), I yet sought for God, hoped that I should find Him, and from old habit addressed prayers to that which I sought but had not found. I went over in my mind the arguments of Kant and Schopenhauer showing the impossibility of proving the existence of a God, and I began to verify those arguments and to refute them. Cause, said I to myself, is not a category of thought such as are Time and Space. If I exist, there must be some cause for it, and a cause of causes. And that first cause of all is what men have called "God." And I paused on that thought, and tried with all my being to recognize the presence of that cause. And as soon as I acknowledged that there is a force in whose power I am, I at once felt that I could live. But I asked myself: What is that cause, that force? How am I to think of it? What are my relations to that which I call "God"? And only the familiar replies occurred to me: "He is the Creator and Preserver." This reply did not satisfy me, and I felt I was losing within me what I needed for my life. I became terrified and began to pray to Him whom I sought, that He should help me. But the more I prayed the more apparent it became to me that He did not hear me, and that there was no one to whom to address myself. And with despair in my heart that there is no God at all, I said: "Lord, have mercy, save me! Lord, teach me!" But no one had mercy on me, and I felt that my life was coming to a standstill.

But again and again, from various sides, I returned to the same admission that I could not have come into the world without any cause or reason or meaning; I could not be such a fledgling fallen from its nest as I felt myself to be. Or, granting that I be such, lying on my back crying in the high grass, even then I cry because I know that a mother has borne me within her, has hatched me, warmed me, fed me, and loved me. Where is she—that mother? If I have been deserted, who has deserted me? I cannot hide from myself that some one bore me, loving me. Who was that some one? Again "God"? He knows and sees my searching, my despair, and my struggle."

"He exists," said I to myself. And I had only for an instant to admit that, and at once life rose within me, and I felt the possibility and joy of being. But again, from the admission of the existence of a God I went on to seek my relation with Him; and again I imagined *that* God—our Creator in Three Persons who sent His Son, the Saviour— and again *that* God, detached from the world and from me, melted like a block of ice, melted before my eyes, and again nothing remained, and again the spring of life dried up within me, and I despaired, and felt that I had nothing to do but to kill myself. And the worst of all was, that I felt I could not do it.

Not twice or three times, but tens and hundreds of times, I reached those conditions, first of joy and animation, and then of despair and consciousness of the impossibility of living.

I remember that it was in early spring: I was alone in the wood listening to its sounds. I listened and thought ever of the same thing, as I had constantly done during those last three years. I was again seeking God.

"Very well, there is no God," said I to myself; "there is no one who is not my imagination but a reality like my whole life. He does not exist, and no miracles can prove His existence, because the miracles would be my imagination, besides being irrational.

"But my *perception* of God, of Him whom I seek," asked I of myself, "where has that perception come from?" And again at this thought the glad waves of life rose within me. All that was around me came to life and received a meaning. But my joy did not last long. My mind continued its work.

"The conception of God is not God," said I to myself. "The conception is what takes place within me. The conception of God is something I can evoke or can refrain from evoking in myself. That is not what I seek. I seek that without which there can be no life." And again all around me and within me began to die, and again I wished to kill myself.

But then I turned my gaze upon myself, on what went on within me, and I remembered all those cessations of life and reanimations that recurred within me hundreds of times. I remembered that I only lived at those times when I believed in God. As it was before, so it was now; I need only be aware of God to live; I need only forget Him, or disbelieve in Him, and I died.

What is this animation and dying? I do not live when I lose belief in the existence of God. I should long ago have killed myself had I not had a dim hope of finding Him. I live, really live, only when I feel Him and seek Him. "What more do you seek?" exclaimed a voice within me. "This is He. He is that without which one cannot live. To know God and to live is one and the same thing. God is life."

"Live seeking God, and then you will not live without God." And more than ever before, all within me and around me lit up, and the light did not again abandon me.

And I was saved from suicide. When and how this change occurred I could not say. As imperceptibly and gradually the force of life in me had been destroyed and I had reached the impossibility of living, a cessation of life and the necessity of suicide, so imperceptibly and gradually did that force of life return to me. And strange to say the strength of life which returned to me was not new, but quite old—the same that had borne me along in my earliest days.

I quite returned to what belonged to my earliest childhood and youth. I returned to the belief in that Will which produced me, and desires something of me. I returned to the belief that the chief and only aim of my life is to be better, i.e. to live in accord with that Will. And I returned to the belief that I can find the expression of that Will in what humanity, in the distant past hidden from me, has produced for its guidance: that is to say, I returned to a belief in God, in moral perfection, and in a tradition transmitting the meaning of life. There was only this difference, that then all this was accepted unconsciously, while now I knew that without it I could not live.

What happened to me was something of this kind: I was put into a boat (I do not remember when) and pushed off from an unknown shore, shown the direction of the opposite shore, had oars put into my unpractised hands, and was left alone. I rowed as best I could and moved forward; but the further I advanced towards the middle of the stream the more rapid grew the current bearing me away from my goal, and the more frequently did I encounter others, like myself, borne away by the stream. There were a few rowers who continued to row, there were others who had abandoned their oars; there were large boats and immense vessels full of people. Some struggled against the current, others yielded to it. And the further I went the more I forgot, seeing the progress down the current of all those who were adrift, I forgot the direction given me. In the very centre of the stream, amid the crowd of boats and vessels which were being borne down stream, I quite lost my direction and abandoned my oars. Around me, on all sides, with mirth and rejoicing, people with sails and oars were borne down the stream, assuring me and each other that no other direction was possible. And I believed them and floated with them. And I was carried far; so far that I heard the roar of the rapids in which I must be shattered, and I saw boats shattered in them. And I recollected myself. I was long unable to understand what had happened to me. I saw before me nothing but destruction, towards which I was rushing, and which I feared. I saw no safety anywhere, and did not know what to do; but, looking back, I perceived innumerable boats which unceasingly and strenuously pushed across the stream, and I remembered about the shore, the oars, and the direction, and began to pull back upwards against the stream and towards the shore.

That shore was God; that direction was tradition; the oars were the freedom given me to pull for the shore and unite with God. And so the force of life was renewed in me, and I again began to live.

XIII

I TURNED from the life of our circle, acknowledging that ours is not life, but a simulation of life—that the conditions of superfluity in which we live deprive us of the possibility of understanding life, and that in order to understand life I must understand not an exceptional life such as ours who are parasites on life, but the life of the simple labouring folk—those who make life—and the meaning which they attribute to it. The simplest labouring people around me were the Russian people, and I turned to them, and to the meaning of life which they give. That meaning, if one can put it into words, was as follows: Every man has come into this world by the will of God. And God has so made man that every man can destroy his soul or save it. The aim of man in life is to save his soul, and to save his soul he must live "godly" and to live "godly" he must renounce all the pleasures of life, must labour, humble himself, suffer and be merciful. That meaning the people obtain from the whole teaching of faith transmitted to them by their pastors and by the traditions that live among the people. This meaning was clear to me and near to my heart. But together with this meaning of the popular faith of our non-sectarian folk, among whom I live, much was inseparably bound up that revolted me and seemed to me inexplicable: sacraments, Church services, fasts, and the adoration of relics and icons. The people cannot separate the one from the other, nor could I. And strange as much of what entered into the faith of these people was to me, I accepted everything; and attended the services, knelt morning and evening in prayer, fasted, and prepared to receive the Eucharist: and at first my reason did not resist anything. The very things that had formerly seemed to me impossible did not now evoke in me any opposition.

My relations to faith before and after were quite different. Formerly life itself seemed to me full of meaning, and faith presented itself as the arbitrary assertion of propositions to me quite unnecessary, unreasonable, and disconnected from life. I then asked myself what meaning those propositions had and, convinced that they had none, I rejected them. Now on the contrary I knew firmly that my life otherwise has, and can have, no meaning; and the articles of faith were far from presenting themselves to me as unnecessary—on the contrary I had been led by indubitable experience to the conviction that only these propositions presented by faith give life a meaning. Formerly I looked on them as on some quite unnecessary gibberish, but now, if I did not understand them, I yet knew that they had a meaning, and I said to myself that I must learn to understand them.

I argued as follows, telling myself that the knowledge of faith flows, like all humanity with its reason, from a mysterious source. That source is God, the origin both of the human body and the human reason. As my body has descended to me from God, so also has my reason and my understanding of life, and consequently the various stages of the development of that understanding of life cannot be false. All that people sincerely believe in must be true; it may be differently expressed but it cannot be a lie, and therefore if it presents itself to me as a lie, that only means that I have not understood it. Furthermore I said to myself, the essence of every faith consists in its giving life a meaning which death does not destroy. Naturally for a faith to be able to reply to the questions of a king dying in luxury, of an old slave tormented by overwork, of an unreasonable child, of a wise old man, of a half-witted old woman, of a young and happy wife, of a youth tormented by passions, of all people in the most varied conditions of life and education—if there is one reply to the one eternal question of life: "Why do I live, and what will result from my life?"—the reply, though one in its essence, must be endlessly varied in its presentation, and the more it is one, the more true and profound it is, the more strange and deformed must it naturally appear in its attempted expression, conformably to the education and position of each person. But this argument, justifying in my eyes the queerness of much on the ritual side of religion, did not suffice to allow me in the one great affair of life—religion—to do things which seemed to me questionable. With all my soul I wished to be in a position to mingle with the people, fulfilling the ritual side of their religion; but I could not do it. I felt that I should lie to myself, and mock at what was sacred to me, were I to do so. At this point, however, our new Russian theological writers came to my rescue.

According to the explanation these theologians gave, the fundamental dogma of our faith is the infallibility of the Church. From the admission of that dogma follows inevitably the truth of all that is professed by the Church. The Church as an assembly of true believers united by love, and therefore possessed of true knowledge, became the basis of my belief. I told myself that divine truth cannot be accessible to a separate individual; it is revealed only to the whole assembly of people united by love. To attain truth one must not separate; and in order not to separate, one must love and must endure things one may not agree with.

Truth reveals itself to love, and if you do not submit to the rites of the Church, you transgress against love; and by transgressing against love you deprive yourself of the possibility of recognizing the truth. I did not then see the sophistry contained in this argument. I did not see that union in love may give the greatest love, but certainly cannot give us divine truth expressed in the definite words of the Nicene Creed. I also did not perceive that love cannot make a certain expression of truth an obligatory condition of union. I did not then see these mistakes in the argument and, thanks to it, was able to accept and perform all the rites of the Orthodox Church without understanding most of them. I then tried with all the strength of my soul to avoid all arguments and contradictions, and tried to explain as reasonably as possible the statements of the Church I encountered.

When fulfilling the rites of the Church, I humbled my reason and submitted to the tradition possessed by all humanity. I united myself with my forefathers: the father, mother, and grandparents I loved. They and all my predecessors believed and lived, and they produced me. I united myself also with the millions of the common people, whom I respected. Moreover, those actions had nothing bad in themselves ("bad" I considered the indulgence of one's desires). When rising early for Church services, I knew I was doing well, if only because I was sacrificing my bodily ease to humble my mental pride, for the sake of union with my ancestors and contemporaries, and for the sake of finding the meaning of life. It was the same with my preparations to receive Communion, and with the daily reading of prayers with genuflections, and also with the observance of all the fasts. However insignificant these sacrifices might be, I made them for the sake of something good. I fasted, prepared for Communion, and observed the fixed hours of prayer at home and in church. During Church service I attended to every word, and gave them a meaning whenever I could. In the Mass the most important words for me were: "Let us love one another in conformity!" The further words, "In unity we believe, in the Father, the Son, and Holy Ghost," I passed by, because I could not understand them.

XIV

IT was then so necessary for me to believe in order to live that I unconsciously concealed from myself the contradictions and obscurities of theology. But this reading of meanings into the rites had its limits. If the chief words in the prayer for the Emperor became more and more clear to me, if I found some explanation for the words "and remembering our Sovereign Most-Holy Mother of God and all the Saints, ourselves and one another, we give our whole life to Christ our God," if I explained to myself the frequent repetition of prayers for the Tsar and his relations by the fact that they are more exposed to temptations than other people and therefore are more in need of being prayed for—the prayers about subduing our enemies and evil under our feet (even if one tried to say that *sin* was the enemy prayed against), these and other prayers, such as the "cherubic song" and the whole sacrament of the oblation, or "the chosen warriors," etc.—quite two-thirds of all the services—either remained completely incomprehensible or, when I forced an explanation into them, made me feel that I was lying, thereby quite destroying my relation to God and depriving me of all possibility of belief.

I felt the same about the celebration of the chief holidays. To remember the Sabbath, that is to devote one day to God, was something I could understand. But the chief holiday was in commemoration of the Resurrection, the reality of which I could not picture to myself or understand. And that name of "Resurrection" was also given to the weekly holiday.[1] And on those days the Sacrament of the Eucharist was administered, which was quite unintelligible to me. The rest of the twelve great holidays, except Christmas, commemorated miracles—the things I tried not to think about in order not to deny: the Ascension, Pentecost, Epiphany, the Feast of the Intercession of the Holy Virgin, etc. At the celebration of these holidays, feeling that importance was being attributed to the very things that to me presented a negative importance, I either devised tranquillizing explanations or shut my eyes in order not to see what tempted me.

Most of all this happened to me when taking part in the most usual Sacraments, which are considered the most important: baptism and communion. There I encountered not incomprehensible but fully comprehensible doings:

---

[1] In Russia Sunday is called Resurrection-day.

doings which seemed to me to lead into temptation, and I was in a dilemma—whether to lie, or to reject them.

Never shall I forge the painful feeling I experienced the day I received the Eucharist for the first time after many years. The service, confession, and prayers were quite intelligible and produced in me a glad consciousness that the meaning of life was being revealed to me. The Communion itself I explained as an act performed in remembrance of Christ, and indicating a purification from sin and the full acceptance of Christ's teaching. If that explanation was artificial I did not notice its artificiality: so happy was I at humbling and abasing myself before the priest—a simple, timid country clergyman—turning all the dirt out of my soul and confessing my vices, so glad was I to merge in thought with the humility of the fathers who wrote the prayers of the office, so glad was I of union with all who have believed and now believe, that I did not notice the artificiality of my explanation. But when I approached the altar gates, and the priest made me say that I believed that what I was about to swallow was truly flesh and blood, I felt a pain in my heart: it was not merely a false note, it was a cruel demand made by some one or other who evidently had never known what faith is.

I now permit myself to say that it was a cruel demand, but I did not then think so: only it was indescribably painful to me. I was no longer in the position in which I had been in youth, when I thought all in life was clear; I had indeed come to faith because, apart from faith, I had found nothing, certainly nothing, except destruction; therefore to throw away that faith was impossible, and I submitted. And I found in my soul a feeling which helped me to endure it. This was the feeling of self-abasement and humility. I humbled myself, swallowed that flesh and blood without any blasphemous feelings, and with a wish to believe. But the blow had been struck and, knowing what awaited me, I could not go a second time.

I continued to fulfil the rites of the Church and still believed that the doctrine I was following contained the truth, when something happened to me which I now understand but which then seemed strange.

I was listening to the conversation of an illiterate peasant, a pilgrim, about God, faith, life, and salvation, when a knowledge of faith revealed itself to me. I drew near to the people, listening to their opinions of life and faith, and I understood the truth more and more. So also was it when I read the Lives of Holy Men, which became my favourite books. Putting aside the miracles, and regarding them as fables illustrating thoughts, this reading revealed to me life's meaning. There were the lives of Makarius the Great, the story of Buddha, there were the words of St. John Chrysostom, and there were the stories of the traveller in the well, the monk who found some gold, and of Peter the publican. There were stories of the martyrs, all announcing that death does not exclude life; and there were the stories of ignorant, stupid men, who knew nothing of the teaching of the Church, but who yet were saved.

But as soon as I met learned believers, or took up their books, doubt of myself, dissatisfaction, and exasperated disputation were roused within me, and I felt that the more I entered into the meaning of these men's speech, the more I went astray from truth and approached an abyss.

XV

How often I envied the peasants their illiteracy and lack of learning! Those statements in the creeds, which to me were evident absurdities, for them contained nothing false; they could accept them and could believe in the truth—in the truth I believed in. Only to me, unhappy man, was it clear that with truth falsehood was interwoven by finest threads, and that I could not accept it in that form.

So I lived for about three years. At first, when I was only slightly associated with truth as a catechumen, and was only scenting out what seemed to me clearest, these encounters struck me less. When I did not understand anything, I said, "It is my fault, I am sinful"; but the more I became imbued with the truths I was learning, the more they became the basis of my life, the more oppressive and the more painful became these encounters, and the sharper became the line between what I do not under- stand because I am not able to understand it, and what cannot be understood except by lying to oneself.

In spite of my doubts and sufferings I still clung to the Orthodox Church. But questions of life arose which had to be decided; and the decision of these questions by the Church—contrary to the very bases of the belief by which I lived—obliged me at last to renounce communion with Orthodoxy as impossible. These questions were: first the relation of the Orthodox Eastern Church to other Churches—to the Catholics and to the so-called sectari- ans. At that time, in consequence of my interest in religion, I came into touch with believers of various faiths: Catholics, Protestants, Old-Believers, Molokans,[1] and others. And I met among them many men of lofty morals who were truly religious. I wished to be a brother to them. And what happened? That teaching which promised to unite all in one faith and love—that very teaching, in the person of

---

[1] A sect that rejects sacraments and ritual.

its best representatives, told me that these men were all
living a lie; that what gave them their power of life was a
temptation of the devil; and what we alone possess the only
possible truth. And I saw that all who do not profess an
identical faith with themselves are considered by the
Orthodox to be heretics; just as the Catholics and others
consider the Orthodox to be heretics. And I saw that the
Orthodox (though they try to hide this) regard with hostility all who do not express their faith by the same external
symbols and words as themselves; and this is naturally so;
first, because the assertion that you are in falsehood and I
am in truth, is the most cruel thing one man can say to
another; and secondly, because a man loving his children
and brothers cannot help being hostile to those who wish
to pervert his children and brothers to a false belief. And
that hostility is increased in proportion to one's greater
knowledge of theology. And to me, who considered that
truth lay in union by love, it became self-evident that theology was itself destroying what it ought to produce.

This temptation is so obvious to us educated people who
have lived in countries where various religions are professed, and have seen the contempt, self-assurance, and
invincible contradiction with which Catholics behave to
the Orthodox Greeks and to the Protestants, and the
Orthodox to Catholics and Protestants, and the Protestants
to the two others, and the similar attitude of Old-Believers,
Pashkovites (Russian Evangelicals), Shakers, and all religions—that the very obviousness of the temptation at first
perplexes us. One says to oneself: it is impossible that it is
so simple and that people do not see that if two assertions
are mutually contradictory, then neither of them has the
sole truth which faith should possess. There is something
else here, there must be some explanation. I thought there

was, and sought that explanation, and read all I could on the subject, and consulted all whom I could. And no one gave me any explanation, except the one which causes the Sumsky Hussars to consider the Sumsky Hussars the best regiment in the world, and the Yellow Uhlans to consider that the best regiment in the world is the Yellow Uhlans. The ecclesiastics of all the different creeds, through their best representatives, told me nothing but that they believed themselves to have the truth and the others to be in error, and that all they could do was to pray for them. I went to archimandrites, bishops, elders, monks of the strictest orders, and asked them; but none of them made any attempt to explain the matter to me, except one man, who explained it all, and explained it so that I never asked any one any more about it. I said that for every unbeliever turning to a belief (and all our young generation are in a position to do so) the question that presents itself first is, why is truth not in Lutheranism nor in Catholicism, but in Orthodoxy? Educated in the high school, he cannot help knowing—what the peasants do not know—that the Protestants and Catholics equally affirm that their faith is the only true one. Historical evidence, twisted by each religion in its own favour, is insufficient. Is it not possible, said I, to understand the teaching in a loftier way, so that from its height the differences should disappear, as they do for one who believes truly? Can we not go further along a path like the one we are following with the Old-Believers? They emphasize the fact that they have a differently shaped cross and different alleluias and a different procession round the altar. We reply: You believe in the Nicene Creed, in the seven sacraments, and so do we. Let us hold to that, and in other matters do as you please. We have united with them by placing the essentials of faith above the unessentials. Now with the Catholics, can we not say: You believe in so and so and in so and so, which are the chief things, and as for the Filioque clause and the Pope—do as you please. Can we not say the same to the Protestants, uniting with them in what is most important?

My interlocutor agreed with my thoughts, but told me that such concessions would bring reproach on the spiritual authorities for deserting the faith of our forefathers, and this would produce a schism; and the vocation of the spiritual authorities is to safeguard in all its purity the Greco-Russian Orthodox faith inherited from our forefathers.

And I understood it all. I am seeking a faith, the power of life; and they are seeking the best way to fulfil in the eyes of men certain human obligations. And fulfilling these human affairs they fulfil them in a human way. However much they may talk of their pity for their erring brethren, and of addressing prayers for them to the throne of the Almighty—to carry out human purposes violence is necessary, and it has always been applied, and is and will be applied. If of two religions each considers itself true, and the other false, then desiring to attract others to the truth, men will preach their own doctrine. And if a false teaching is preached to the inexperienced sons of their Church—which has the truth—then that Church cannot but burn the books and remove the man who is misleading its sons. What is to be done with a sectarian—burning, in the opinion of the Orthodox, with the fire of false doctrine—who in the most important affair of life, in faith, misleads the sons of the Church? What can be done with him, except to cut off his head, or to incarcerate him? Under the Tsar Alexis Mikhaylovich, people were burned at the stake, that is to say, the severest method of punishment of the time was applied, and in our day also, the severest method of punishment is applied—detention in solitary confinement.[1]

And I turned my attention to what is done in the name of religion and was horrified, and I almost entirely abjured Orthodoxy.

The second relation of the Church to a question of life was with regard to war and executions.

At that time Russia was at war. And Russians, in the name of Christian love, began to kill their fellow men. It was impossible not to think about this, and not to see that killing is an evil repugnant to the first principles of any faith. Yet prayers were said in the churches for the success of our arms, and the teachers of the Faith acknowledged killing to be an act resulting from the Faith. And besides the murders during the war, I saw, during the disturbances which followed the war, Church dignitaries and teachers and monks of the lesser and stricter orders who approved the killing of helpless, erring youths. And I took note of all that is done by men who profess Christianity, and I was horrified.

XVI

And I ceased to doubt, and became fully convinced that not all was true in the religion I had joined. Formerly I should have said that it was all false; but I could not say so now. The whole of the people had a certain a knowledge of the truth, for otherwise they could not have lived. Moreover, that knowledge was accessible to me, for I had

---

[1] At the time this was written, capital punishment was considered to be abolished in Russia.

felt it and had lived by it. But I no longer doubted that there was also falsehood in it. And all that had previously repelled me now presented itself vividly before me. And though I saw that among the peasants there was a smaller admixture of the lies that repelled me than among the representatives of the Church, I still saw that in the people's belief also falsehood was mixed with the truth.

But where did the truth and where did the falsehood come from? Both the falsehood and the truth were contained in the so-called holy tradition and in the Scriptures. Both the falsehood and the truth had been handed down by what is called the Church.

And whether I liked or not, I was brought to the study and investigation of these writings and traditions—which till now I had been so afraid to investigate.

And I turned to the examination of that same theology which I had once rejected with such contempt as unnecessary. Formerly it seemed to me a series of unnecessary absurdities, when on all sides I was surrounded by manifestations of life which seemed to me clear and full of sense; now I should have been glad to throw away what would not enter a healthy head, but I had nowhere to turn to. On this teaching religious doctrine rests, or at least with it the only knowledge of the meaning of life that I have found is inseparably connected. However wild it may seem to my firm old mind, it was the only hope of salvation. It had to be carefully, attentively examined in order to understand it, and not even to understand it as I understand the propositions of science: I do not seek that, nor can I seek it, knowing the peculiarity of the knowledge of faith. I shall not seek the explanation of everything. I know that the explanation of everything, like the commencement of everything, must be concealed in infinity. But I wish to understand in a way which will bring me to what is inevitably inexplicable. I wish to recognize anything that is inexplicable, as being so not because the demands of my reason are wrong (they are right, and apart from them I can understand nothing), but because I recognize the limits of my intellect. I wish to understand in such a way that everything that is inexplicable shall present itself to me as being necessarily inexplicable, and not as being something I am under an arbitrary obligation to believe.

That there is truth in the teaching is to me indubitable; but it is also certain that there is falsehood in it, and I must find what is true and what is false, and must disentangle the one from the other. I am setting to work upon this task. What of falsehood I have found in the teaching, and what I have found of truth, and to what conclusions I came, will form the following parts of this work, which if it be worth it, and if anyone wants it, will probably some day be printed somewhere.

1879.

The foregoing was written by me some three years ago, and will be printed.

Now, a few days ago, when revising it and returning to the line of thought and to the feelings I had when I was living through it all, I had a dream. This dream expressed in condensed form all that I had experienced and described, and I think therefore that, for those who have understood me, a description of this dream will refresh and elucidate and unify what has been set forth at such length in the foregoing pages. The dream was this:—

I saw that I was lying on a bed. I was neither comfortable nor uncomfortable: I was lying on my back. But I began to consider how, and on what, I was lying—a question which had not till then occurred to me. And observing my bed, I saw I was lying on plaited string suspenders attached to its sides: my feet were resting on one such suspender, my calves on another, and my legs felt uncomfortable. I seemed to know that those suspenders were movable, and with a movement of my foot I pushed away the furthest of them at my feet—it seemed to me that it would be more comfortable so. But I pushed it away too far and wished to reach it again with my foot, and that movement caused the next suspender under my calves to slip away also, so that my legs hung in the air. I made a movement with my whole body to adjust myself, fully convinced that I could do so at once; but the movement caused the other suspenders under me to slip and to become entangled, and I saw that matters were going quite wrong: the whole of the lower part of my body slipped and hung down, though my feet did not reach the ground. I was holding on only by the upper part of my back, and not only did it become uncomfortable but I was even frightened. And then only did I ask myself about something that had not before occurred to me. I asked myself: Where am I, and what am I lying on? and I began to look around, and first of all to look down in the direction in which my body was hanging, and whither I felt I must soon fall. I looked down and did not believe my eyes. I was not only at a height comparable to the height of the highest towers or mountains, but at a height such as I could never have imagined.

I could not even make out whether I saw anything there below, in that bottomless abyss over which I was hanging and whither I was being drawn. My heart contracted, and I experienced horror. To look thither was terrible. If I looked thither, I felt that I should at once slip from the last suspender and perish. And I did not look. But not to look was still worse, for I thought of what would happen to me directly I fell from the last suspender. And I felt that from fear I was losing my last supports, and that my back was slowly slipping lower and lower. Another moment and I should drop off. And then it occurred to me that this cannot be real. It is a dream. Wake up! I try to arouse myself but cannot do so. What am I to do? What am I to do? I ask myself, and look upwards. Above, there is also an infinite space. I look into the immensity of sky and try to forget about the immensity below, and I really do forget it. The immensity below, and I really do forget it. The immensity below repels and frightens me; the immensity above attracts and strengthens me. I am still supported above the abyss by the last suspenders that have not yet slipped from under me; I know that I am hanging; but I look only upwards and my fear passes. As happens in dreams, a voice says: "Notice this, this is it!" And I look more and more into the infinite above me and feel that I am becoming calm. I remember all that has happened, and remember how it all happened; how I moved my legs, how I hung down, how frightened I was, and how I was saved from fear by looking upwards. And I ask myself: Well, and now am I not hanging just the same? And I do not so much look round as experience with my whole body the point of support on which I am held. I see that I no longer hang as if about to fall, but am firmly held. I ask myself how I am held: I feel about, look round, and see that under me, under the middle of my body, there is one suspender, and that when I look upwards I lie on it in the position of securest balance, and that it alone gave me support before. And then, as happens in dreams, I imagined the mechanism by means of which I was held; a vey natural, intelligible, and sure means, though to one awake that mechanism has no sense. I, in my dream, was even surprised that I had not understood it sooner. It appeared that at my head there was a pillar, and the security of that slender pillar was undoubted, though there was nothing to support it. From the pillar a loop hung very ingeniously and yet simply, and if one lay with the middle of one's body in that loop and looked up, there could be no question of falling. This was all clear to me, and I was glad and tranquil. And it seemed as if someone said to me: "See that you remember."

And I awoke.

1882.

A CATALOG OF SELECTED

DOVER BOOKS

IN ALL FIELDS OF INTEREST

A CATALOG OF SELECTED DOVER
BOOKS IN ALL FIELDS OF INTEREST

100 BEST-LOVED POEMS, Edited by Philip Smith. "The Passionate Shepherd to His Love," "Shall I compare thee to a summer's day?" "Death, be not proud," "The Raven," "The Road Not Taken," plus works by Blake, Wordsworth, Byron, Shelley, Keats, many others. 96pp. 5³⁄₁₆ x 8¼. 0-486-28553-7

100 SMALL HOUSES OF THE THIRTIES, Brown-Blodgett Company. Exterior photographs and floor plans for 100 charming structures. Illustrations of models accompanied by descriptions of interiors, color schemes, closet space, and other amenities. 200 illustrations. 112pp. 8⅜ x 11. 0-486-44131-8

1000 TURN-OF-THE-CENTURY HOUSES: With Illustrations and Floor Plans, Herbert C. Chivers. Reproduced from a rare edition, this showcase of homes ranges from cottages and bungalows to sprawling mansions. Each house is meticulously illustrated and accompanied by complete floor plans. 256pp. 9⅜ x 12¼.
0-486-45596-3

101 GREAT AMERICAN POEMS, Edited by The American Poetry & Literacy Project. Rich treasury of verse from the 19th and 20th centuries includes works by Edgar Allan Poe, Robert Frost, Walt Whitman, Langston Hughes, Emily Dickinson, T. S. Eliot, other notables. 96pp. 5³⁄₁₆ x 8¼. 0-486-40158-8

101 GREAT SAMURAI PRINTS, Utagawa Kuniyoshi. Kuniyoshi was a master of the warrior woodblock print — and these 18th-century illustrations represent the pinnacle of his craft. Full-color portraits of renowned Japanese samurais pulse with movement, passion, and remarkably fine detail. 112pp. 8⅜ x 11. 0-486-46523-3

ABC OF BALLET, Janet Grosser. Clearly worded, abundantly illustrated little guide defines basic ballet-related terms: arabesque, battement, pas de chat, relevé, sissonne, many others. Pronunciation guide included. Excellent primer. 48pp. 4³⁄₁₆ x 5¾.
0-486-40871-X

ACCESSORIES OF DRESS: An Illustrated Encyclopedia, Katherine Lester and Bess Viola Oerke. Illustrations of hats, veils, wigs, cravats, shawls, shoes, gloves, and other accessories enhance an engaging commentary that reveals the humor and charm of the many-sided story of accessorized apparel. 644 figures and 59 plates. 608pp. 6⅛ x 9¼.
0-486-43378-1

ADVENTURES OF HUCKLEBERRY FINN, Mark Twain. Join Huck and Jim as their boyhood adventures along the Mississippi River lead them into a world of excitement, danger, and self-discovery. Humorous narrative, lyrical descriptions of the Mississippi valley, and memorable characters. 224pp. 5³⁄₁₆ x 8¼. 0-486-28061-6

ALICE STARMORE'S BOOK OF FAIR ISLE KNITTING, Alice Starmore. A noted designer from the region of Scotland's Fair Isle explores the history and techniques of this distinctive, stranded-color knitting style and provides copious illustrated instructions for 14 original knitwear designs. 208pp. 8⅜ x 10⅞. 0-486-47218-3

Browse over 9,000 books at www.doverpublications.com

ALICE'S ADVENTURES IN WONDERLAND, Lewis Carroll. Beloved classic about a little girl lost in a topsy-turvy land and her encounters with the White Rabbit, March Hare, Mad Hatter, Cheshire Cat, and other delightfully improbable characters. 42 illustrations by Sir John Tenniel. 96pp. 5³⁄₁₆ x 8¼.　　　　　　　0-486-27543-4

AMERICA'S LIGHTHOUSES: An Illustrated History, Francis Ross Holland. Profusely illustrated fact-filled survey of American lighthouses since 1716. Over 200 stations — East, Gulf, and West coasts, Great Lakes, Hawaii, Alaska, Puerto Rico, the Virgin Islands, and the Mississippi and St. Lawrence Rivers. 240pp. 8 x 10¾.

0-486-25576-X

AN ENCYCLOPEDIA OF THE VIOLIN, Alberto Bachmann. Translated by Frederick H. Martens. Introduction by Eugene Ysaye. First published in 1925, this renowned reference remains unsurpassed as a source of essential information, from construction and evolution to repertoire and technique. Includes a glossary and 73 illustrations. 496pp. 6½ x 9¼.　　　　　　　0-486-46618-3

ANIMALS: 1,419 Copyright-Free Illustrations of Mammals, Birds, Fish, Insects, etc., Selected by Jim Harter. Selected for its visual impact and ease of use, this outstanding collection of wood engravings presents over 1,000 species of animals in extremely lifelike poses. Includes mammals, birds, reptiles, amphibians, fish, insects, and other invertebrates. 284pp. 9 x 12.　　　　　　　0-486-23766-4

THE ANNALS, Tacitus. Translated by Alfred John Church and William Jackson Brodribb. This vital chronicle of Imperial Rome, written by the era's great historian, spans A.D. 14-68 and paints incisive psychological portraits of major figures, from Tiberius to Nero. 416pp. 5³⁄₁₆ x 8¼.　　　　　　　0-486-45236-0

ANTIGONE, Sophocles. Filled with passionate speeches and sensitive probing of moral and philosophical issues, this powerful and often-performed Greek drama reveals the grim fate that befalls the children of Oedipus. Footnotes. 64pp. 5³⁄₁₆ x 8 ¼.　　　　　　　0-486-27804-2

ART DECO DECORATIVE PATTERNS IN FULL COLOR, Christian Stoll. Reprinted from a rare 1910 portfolio, 160 sensuous and exotic images depict a breathtaking array of florals, geometrics, and abstracts — all elegant in their stark simplicity. 64pp. 8⅜ x 11.　　　　　　　0-486-44862-2

THE ARTHUR RACKHAM TREASURY: 86 Full-Color Illustrations, Arthur Rackham. Selected and Edited by Jeff A. Menges. A stunning treasury of 86 full-page plates span the famed English artist's career, from *Rip Van Winkle* (1905) to masterworks such as *Undine, A Midsummer Night's Dream,* and *Wind in the Willows* (1939). 96pp. 8⅜ x 11.

0-486-44685-9

THE AUTHENTIC GILBERT & SULLIVAN SONGBOOK, W. S. Gilbert and A. S. Sullivan. The most comprehensive collection available, this songbook includes selections from every one of Gilbert and Sullivan's light operas. Ninety-two numbers are presented uncut and unedited, and in their original keys. 410pp. 9 x 12.

0-486-23482-7

THE AWAKENING, Kate Chopin. First published in 1899, this controversial novel of a New Orleans wife's search for love outside a stifling marriage shocked readers. Today, it remains a first-rate narrative with superb characterization. New introductory Note. 128pp. 5³⁄₁₆ x 8¼.　　　　　　　0-486-27786-0

BASIC DRAWING, Louis Priscilla. Beginning with perspective, this commonsense manual progresses to the figure in movement, light and shade, anatomy, drapery, composition, trees and landscape, and outdoor sketching. Black-and-white illustrations throughout. 128pp. 8⅜ x 11.　　　　　　　0-486-45815-6

THE BATTLES THAT CHANGED HISTORY, Fletcher Pratt. Historian profiles 16 crucial conflicts, ancient to modern, that changed the course of Western civilization. Gripping accounts of battles led by Alexander the Great, Joan of Arc, Ulysses S. Grant, other commanders. 27 maps. 352pp. 5⅜ x 8½. 0-486-41129-X

BEETHOVEN'S LETTERS, Ludwig van Beethoven. Edited by Dr. A. C. Kalischer. Features 457 letters to fellow musicians, friends, greats, patrons, and literary men. Reveals musical thoughts, quirks of personality, insights, and daily events. Includes 15 plates. 410pp. 5⅜ x 8½. 0-486-22769-3

BERNICE BOBS HER HAIR AND OTHER STORIES, F. Scott Fitzgerald. This brilliant anthology includes 6 of Fitzgerald's most popular stories: "The Diamond as Big as the Ritz," the title tale, "The Offshore Pirate," "The Ice Palace," "The Jelly Bean," and "May Day." 176pp. 5⅜ x 8½. 0-486-47049-0

BESLER'S BOOK OF FLOWERS AND PLANTS: 73 Full-Color Plates from Hortus Eystettensis, 1613, Basilius Besler. Here is a selection of magnificent plates from the *Hortus Eystettensis*, which vividly illustrated and identified the plants, flowers, and trees that thrived in the legendary German garden at Eichstätt. 80pp. 8⅜ x 11. 0-486-46005-3

THE BOOK OF KELLS, Edited by Blanche Cirker. Painstakingly reproduced from a rare facsimile edition, this volume contains full-page decorations, portraits, illustrations, plus a sampling of textual leaves with exquisite calligraphy and ornamentation. 32 full-color illustrations. 32pp. 9⅜ x 12¼. 0-486-24345-1

THE BOOK OF THE CROSSBOW: With an Additional Section on Catapults and Other Siege Engines, Ralph Payne-Gallwey. Fascinating study traces history and use of crossbow as military and sporting weapon, from Middle Ages to modern times. Also covers related weapons: balistas, catapults, Turkish bows, more. Over 240 illustrations. 400pp. 7¼ x 10⅛. 0-486-28720-3

THE BUNGALOW BOOK: Floor Plans and Photos of 112 Houses, 1910, Henry L. Wilson. Here are 112 of the most popular and economic blueprints of the early 20th century — plus an illustration or photograph of each completed house. A wonderful time capsule that still offers a wealth of valuable insights. 160pp. 8⅜ x 11. 0-486-45104-6

THE CALL OF THE WILD, Jack London. A classic novel of adventure, drawn from London's own experiences as a Klondike adventurer, relating the story of a heroic dog caught in the brutal life of the Alaska Gold Rush. Note. 64pp. 5³⁄₁₆ x 8¼. 0-486-26472-6

CANDIDE, Voltaire. Edited by Francois-Marie Arouet. One of the world's great satires since its first publication in 1759. Witty, caustic skewering of romance, science, philosophy, religion, government — nearly all human ideals and institutions. 112pp. 5³⁄₁₆ x 8¼. 0-486-26689-3

CELEBRATED IN THEIR TIME: Photographic Portraits from the George Grantham Bain Collection, Edited by Amy Pastan. With an Introduction by Michael Carlebach. Remarkable portrait gallery features 112 rare images of Albert Einstein, Charlie Chaplin, the Wright Brothers, Henry Ford, and other luminaries from the worlds of politics, art, entertainment, and industry. 128pp. 8⅜ x 11. 0-486-46754-6

CHARIOTS FOR APOLLO: The NASA History of Manned Lunar Spacecraft to 1969, Courtney G. Brooks, James M. Grimwood, and Loyd S. Swenson, Jr. This illustrated history by a trio of experts is the definitive reference on the Apollo spacecraft and lunar modules. It traces the vehicles' design, development, and operation in space. More than 100 photographs and illustrations. 576pp. 6¾ x 9¼. 0-486-46756-2

Browse over 9,000 books at www.doverpublications.com

A CHRISTMAS CAROL, Charles Dickens. This engrossing tale relates Ebenezer Scrooge's ghostly journeys through Christmases past, present, and future and his ultimate transformation from a harsh and grasping old miser to a charitable and compassionate human being. 80pp. 5³⁄₁₆ x 8¼.　　　　　　　0-486-26865-9

COMMON SENSE, Thomas Paine. First published in January of 1776, this highly influential landmark document clearly and persuasively argued for American separation from Great Britain and paved the way for the Declaration of Independence. 64pp. 5³⁄₁₆ x 8¼.　　　　　　　0-486-29602-4

THE COMPLETE SHORT STORIES OF OSCAR WILDE, Oscar Wilde. Complete texts of "The Happy Prince and Other Tales," "A House of Pomegranates," "Lord Arthur Savile's Crime and Other Stories," "Poems in Prose," and "The Portrait of Mr. W. H." 208pp. 5³⁄₁₆ x 8¼.　　　　　　　0-486-45216-6

COMPLETE SONNETS, William Shakespeare. Over 150 exquisite poems deal with love, friendship, the tyranny of time, beauty's evanescence, death, and other themes in language of remarkable power, precision, and beauty. Glossary of archaic terms. 80pp. 5³⁄₁₆ x 8¼.　　　　　　　0-486-26686-9

THE COUNT OF MONTE CRISTO: Abridged Edition, Alexandre Dumas. Falsely accused of treason, Edmond Dantès is imprisoned in the bleak Chateau d'If. After a hair-raising escape, he launches an elaborate plot to extract a bitter revenge against those who betrayed him. 448pp. 5³⁄₁₆ x 8¼.　　　　　　　0-486-45643-9

CRAFTSMAN BUNGALOWS: Designs from the Pacific Northwest, Yoho & Merritt. This reprint of a rare catalog, showcasing the charming simplicity and cozy style of Craftsman bungalows, is filled with photos of completed homes, plus floor plans and estimated costs. An indispensable resource for architects, historians, and illustrators. 112pp. 10 x 7.　　　　　　　0-486-46875-5

CRAFTSMAN BUNGALOWS: 59 Homes from "The Craftsman," Edited by Gustav Stickley. Best and most attractive designs from Arts and Crafts Movement publication — 1903–1916 — includes sketches, photographs of homes, floor plans, descriptive text. 128pp. 8¼ x 11.　　　　　　　0-486-25829-7

CRIME AND PUNISHMENT, Fyodor Dostoyevsky. Translated by Constance Garnett. Supreme masterpiece tells the story of Raskolnikov, a student tormented by his own thoughts after he murders an old woman. Overwhelmed by guilt and terror, he confesses and goes to prison. 480pp. 5³⁄₁₆ x 8¼.　　　　　　　0-486-41587-2

THE DECLARATION OF INDEPENDENCE AND OTHER GREAT DOCUMENTS OF AMERICAN HISTORY: 1775-1865, Edited by John Grafton. Thirteen compelling and influential documents: Henry's "Give Me Liberty or Give Me Death," Declaration of Independence, The Constitution, Washington's First Inaugural Address, The Monroe Doctrine, The Emancipation Proclamation, Gettysburg Address, more. 64pp. 5³⁄₁₆ x 8¼.　　　　　　　0-486-41124-9

THE DESERT AND THE SOWN: Travels in Palestine and Syria, Gertrude Bell. "The female Lawrence of Arabia," Gertrude Bell wrote captivating, perceptive accounts of her travels in the Middle East. This intriguing narrative, accompanied by 160 photos, traces her 1905 sojourn in Lebanon, Syria, and Palestine. 368pp. 5⅜ x 8½.
　　　　　　　0-486-46876-3

A DOLL'S HOUSE, Henrik Ibsen. Ibsen's best-known play displays his genius for realistic prose drama. An expression of women's rights, the play climaxes when the central character, Nora, rejects a smothering marriage and life in "a doll's house." 80pp. 5³⁄₁₆ x 8¼.　　　　　　　0-486-27062-9